Rose to the Occasion

An Easy-Growing Guide to Rose Gardening

Easy-Growing Gardening Guide, Vol. 2

Melinda R. "Rosefiend" Cordell

Rosefiend Publishing.

ISBN: 1540690504
ISBN-13: 978-1540690500

**For more information (and more books), visit
www.melindacordell.com**

DEDICATION

To Brad, Sophie, and Stevie
as always

The Rose Family
by Robert Frost

The rose is a rose,
And was always a rose.
But the theory now goes
That the apple's a rose,
And the pear is, and so's
The plum, I suppose.
The dear only knows
What will next prove a rose.
You, of course, are a rose –
But were always a rose.

Table of Contents

INTRODUCTION 1

CHOOSING THE BEST ROSE 5

GROWING HEALTHY ROSES 10

    Choosing and Preparing a Planting Site 10

    The Importance of Soilbuilding 13

SHOPPING FOR ROSES 16

    How to Buy Bare-Root Roses 16

    How to Dig a Hole 20

    What To Look For In Container-Grown Roses 26

    Buying and Planting Roses in the Fall 29

    How to Transplant a Rose 31

CARING FOR ROSES 33

    Watering: Give Roses a Good Long Drink 33

    Mulching: Saving Roots and Plants for Millenia 35

    Fertilizing: Feed the Rose and Feed the Soil 37

    Compost Basics 40

Great Organic Fertilizers for Roses..42

PRUNING AND TRAINING..47

Deadheading..47

ROSE TIPS THROUGH THE YEAR...49

Rose Tips for High Summer..49

November Rose Care..52

Winterize Your Roses..54

SOLVING ROSE-GROWING PROBLEMS...58

Fungicides – Because an Ounce of Prevention etc. etc...........................58

Spot-Spraying Insects is Best...62

Tips For When You Spray...64

Vinegar Makes a Good Herbicide – Just Use the Right Kind..................67

A GALLERY OF BENEFICIAL INSECTS..69

Lacewings (Chrysoperla carnea)..69

Ladybugs (Coccinellidae)..70

Wheel Bugs (Arilus cristatus)...71

Praying Mantis (*Mantis religiosa*)..72

A ROGUE'S GALLERY O' BAD ARTHROPODS......................................73

Spotted Cucumber Beetles...73

Spider Mites..73

Aphids...74

Thrips..76

Japanese Beetles 77

Leaf-Cutter Bees 80

Birds Are On Your Side 81

Rose Rosette Disease: No Cure 83

When a Rose Doesn't Bloom 87

PROPAGATION 88

Rooting Old Roses 88

MONTH-BY-MONTH CHECKLISTS 94

JANUARY 94

FEBRUARY 97

MARCH 98

APRIL 100

MAY 102

JUNE 104

JULY 106

AUGUST 108

SEPTEMBER 110

OCTOBER 112

NOVEMBER 114

Appendix 118

ANTIQUE ROSE SOURCES 120

ABOUT THE AUTHOR 136

ACKNOWLEDGMENTS

A million thanks to the late Charles Anctil, ARS Master Rosarian at Moffet's Nursery, for looking over this manuscript and offering suggestions (all of which I took). You were a damn good rosarian and a good friend.

Founded . . 1850
Incorporated . . 1875

❧ ❧ ❧ ❧ 29th Year in Special Culture of Roses.

INTRODUCTION

When I started working as city horticulturist, I took care of a bunch of gardens around the city, including the big Krug Park rose garden. It included a bunch of the usual scrawny tea roses, some shrub roses, and a bunch of bare ground.

I was more of a perennials gal, but when I looked at the roses, some of them were really nice. The 'Carefree Delight' roses were covered with rumpled pink blossoms. There was a tall 'Mr. Lincoln' rose and some 'Double Delights' that smelled amazing. A bunch of 'Scarlet Meidilands' were really putting on a blooming show, with tiny scarlet flowers cascading all over them. Not shabby at all.

I started taking care of the roses, but along the way I noticed that a lot of the 'Scarlet Meidilands' were sprouting odd growths. Most of the new growth looked fine, with bronzed, flat leaves that looked attractive. But some of the new growth was markedly different – skinny, stunted leaves with pebbled surfaces, and hyperthorny canes that were downright rubbery. The blossoms on these shoots were crinkled and didn't open worth a darn.

I hollered at Charles Anctil, a Master Rosarian with the American Rose Society. We'd known each other since 1992 when we both worked at the Old Mill Nursery. He'd been working with roses for a good 50 years, so he knows his stuff. At any rate, Charles looked over the roses and told me that those roses, and others, had rose rosette virus, a highly contagious disease, and a death sentence for a rose. Every one of those roses had to come out. He couldn't believe the extent of the damage. He said that he had never seen so many roses infected by rose rosette in one place.

Oh great! Why do I get to be the lucky one?

I dug up many roses that spring. In winter, I got a work crew and dug up 50 more. I had to replace all those roses, so I started researching new varieties.

As city horticulturist, I was already running like hell everywhere I went, so I wanted roses that wouldn't wilt or croak or wrap themselves in blackspot every time I looked at them cross-eyed. I wanted tough roses, roses that took heat and drought and bug attacks and zombie apocalypses with aplomb and would still come out looking great and covered with scented blossoms. (And the blossoms HAD to be scented – there was no two ways about that.)

I started reading rose catalogs. I talked to Charles some more, which is always fun. Somewhere along the way, I got obsessed. I immersed myself in roses. That's how I learn – I get excited about a subject and start reading everything in sight about it, like it's a mini-course in school. I read about antique roses, which were making a comeback. Different rose breeders, most notably David Austin, were crossing modern varieties with old varieties and getting roses that combined the best of the new and the old. Other breeders were creating roses that were tough and disease-resistant.

I planted some antique roses, and they looked great. I planted more. The rose garden was really starting to look spiffy, even though I still had to take roses out every year due to the rose rosette virus. I even tucked in some annuals and perennials around the garden to doll up the place when the roses conked out in July and August.

Roses are amazing plants. Many old roses have a long and storied history. Some species that were growing during the time of the Pyramids are still blooming today. And these roses are attractive and fragrant. What could be better?

Some people say that you can't grow roses organically. I say you can. I did use a few chemicals when I was a horticulturist, but that was because I had a huge list of things to do in a limited amount of time. I used Round Up for spot-weeding (a tiny squirt for each weed, just enough to wet the leaves), a systemic granular fungicide to keep up with blackspot, and Miracle-Gro as part of the fertilizing regimen for convenience.

If you choose to use chemicals, use them responsibly. Don't spray them and expect the problem to be fixed. They work best when you combine them with other control methods. I'll give you an example that's not rose-related. I had a mandevilla in the greenhouse that had a huge mealybug problem. (Mealybugs are a small, white insect that sucks out plant juices. The young bugs look like bits of cotton. Picture to the right.) I sprayed the  plant with insecticide until the leaves were dripping. The mealybugs were still there. I put a systemic insecticide around the roots of the plant and watered it in. The mealybugs didn't care.

So I just started squishing the mealybugs with my fingers, a gross job because they squirt orange goo. At that point, I didn't care. I searched them out and squashed them where they were cuddled up around buds, in the cracks of the plant, and under the leaves. I even found some on the roots just under the soil. I squished those and added a little extra potting soil. I checked the plant every other day and squished every mealybug I could find. After a while, I stopped finding them altogether. Then I fertilized the plant, and the mandevilla put out leaves like crazy and started blooming. Success!

Chemicals aren't a cure-all by any means. They're convenient, but sometimes you just have to get in and do a little hands-on work with the plant to help it along. It's a good feeling when a plant you've been working with rights itself and perks up again.

Though I'm no longer a horticulturist, I wrote this book because I have worked in horticulture for about half my life, and have a decent understanding about how the natural world works. I might possibly be just a little crazy about roses. I hope my experiences are helpful and that you're able to benefit from them – and that your roses benefit as well.

P.S. I generally read rose books just so I can look at rose pictures and also check out new varieties. I'm sorry that this book doesn't have any rose pictures in color, because that would have made this book much more expensive. However! **In the Kindle version of this book, ALL THE ROSE PICTURES WILL BE IN COLOR.** I'll add extra pictures of some of my favorite roses, too.

I hope that helps. It's all part of my value-added service.

'Mme. Plantier,' a hybrid alba from 1835, grows to an enormous size but has nearly thornless canes and white, fragrant blossoms.

CHOOSING THE BEST ROSE

The roses that are tops in my book are vigorous, disease-resistant, and sport plenty of scented blossoms. (I don't think I've ever recommended an unscented rose – there's just something wrong with that.) Also to be commended are hardy roses that will take winter's cold, and disease-resistant roses that don't need much spraying. Here are a few good, no-nonsense roses that can take the worst of what nature dishes out and still look amazing.

(Do remember that all my recommendations are suitable for Zones 5-6. If you are farther afield, or overseas, you might ask a local rosarian for recommendations that are best suited to your climate.)

'Carefree Beauty,' bred in 1977, is one of the first roses to bloom in spring. It sports a cloud of large, rumpled, bright pink blossoms through most of the season. This rose is a solid performer through times of drought and is resistant to blackspot and powdery mildew. In the fall, after you stop deadheading the rose, you will be rewarded with large, orange hips. (On the *rose*, not on your body.) "Carefree Beauty" grows about 5 feet tall and wide.

'Blanc Double de Coubert' (say: koo-BEAR), 1892, is a rugosa rose. Rugosas are descended from *Rosa rugosa*, a hardy species rose native to China, Korea, and Japan. Rugosas are tough, able to grow in sand, and can withstand salty sea winds that burn other plants. 'Blanc' grows to about 3 feet tall and covers itself with white blossoms that have a clove-like scent. The thorns on this rose are abundant and sharp. One drawback to 'Blanc': It wants to rule the world, and will sucker freely – that is, its roots will send up a lot of shoots. If you don't keep these suckers under control, your yard may become one big 'Blanc'. Simply mowing them down should do the trick.

'Hansa,' 1905, another rugosa, has deep crimson-purple flowers with a delicious scent. It grows about four feet tall and makes a delightful addition to the garden. Both of these rugosa roses make good hedges, which is why rugosas are sometimes called "hedge roses."

'Therese Bugnet' is pronounced boozh-NAY, not bug-net. Therese is hardy to Zone 3, so she won't need a lot of winter protection. She is also an early bloomer, covering herself in frothy pink roses in May. 'Therese' grows 5 to 6 feet tall and has red stems that offer some winter color. However, she is susceptible to powdery mildew, a fungus that turns the leaves a powdery white color.

'William Baffin' (1983) is one of the roses from the Canadian Explorers series, bred to withstand winters in

Ottawa (Zone 3), so you can bet our paltry winters will be no trouble for it. The roses in the Canadian Explorers series are named for explorers that forged their way into lands where Native Americans and First Nations had lived for thousands of years, then claimed they'd discovered them and stole them away. Well, it's true. Colonialism aside, the Explorer series are all tough, rugged roses that will take extremely cold conditions with no problem.

My 'William Baffin' (I call him "Billy") didn't bloom the first two years, which had me worried. On the third year, however, he covered himself with buds which opened into strawberry-pink blossoms with a few white lines up the center of the petals, and gold stamens in the center of the flower. Vigorous is a mild word for 'William Baffin.' The canes are tall and thick. If you want to prune the rose, bring the tree loppers – heck, bring a tree saw or a chainsaw! Your hand-held pruners won't be big enough for some of these canes even after only a few years in the ground. His thorns will grab you, however careful you are. The rose is quite disease-resistant, always a plus.

I'm not a fan of hybrid teas, which are wimpy in winter and often have unscented blossoms. When I was horticulturing all over the city, I absolutely required my roses to be tough, non-nonsense plants that could take care of themselves, so I mostly rejected hybrid teas. That said, I did plant several hybrid roses because of their lovely fragrance, and they hold up very well in a rose garden with a minimum of fussbudgeting. 'Tiffany' has pink blossoms with yellow in their centers, and a gorgeous smell. 'Double Delight,' with creamy red and white blossoms, just about knocks you down with its scent. I would stick my nose in this rose at every opportunity. I also like the tall and stately 'Mr. Lincoln' (bright red) and 'Angel Face' (ruffled, purple blossoms – and it's not a dog as so many "blue" roses are).

Some of my favorite roses are the old roses that bloom once a year. That's not so bad. Lilacs bloom once a year, too, but we don't kick them out of the garden for it. The old roses cover themselves with blossoms that smell heavenly. Get 'Autumn Damask' (which has been grown since the poet Virgil was alive), 'Roseraie de L'Hay', 'Madame Isaac Pereire' (she gets a little blackspot and mildew – but her flowers more than make up for it in fragrance), 'Madame Pierre Oger', and 'Paul Neyron' (raspberry pink, fragrant blossoms that get huge!).

So many other roses deserve mention. 'The Fairy' is a Polyantha rose that covers herself with tiny pink blossoms. Many of the roses developed by David Austin – which include 'Graham Thomas' and 'Gertrude Jekyll' – are lovely roses, but they don't seem to do as well in the Midwest as these other roses. Somebody once stated that there's no runway between the British Isles and America. That is, a rose that does well in England or Wales might not grow worth a nickel in America, and vice versa.

For best results, visit local rose gardens and talk with rosarians about what they like best. Often they'll suggest a rose variety that will surprise and delight you.

For great overall rose advice, a list of 50 of the best easy growing roses, and a ton of mouth-watering rose pictures, pick up a copy of *The Rose Bible* by the late Rayford Clayton Reddell. His books are all out of print (a travesty!), but you can still get used copies online. I used this book when I was replacing the dead roses at Krug Park, and every rose listed in Reddell's top 50 turned out to be a winner in the garden.

HON. EDITH GIFFORD (H.T.)

'Hon. Edith Gifford,' (1882) a white hybrid tea, is a lovely rose from Gertrude Jekyll's book, very popular at the turn of the century. I cannot find any indication that this particular variety has survived through the years. (However, if anybody has seen one, do let me know – I'd love to see what this rose looks like in color. She might simply be going by another name these days)

GROWING HEALTHY ROSES

Choosing and Preparing a Planting Site

So the very first order of business is deciding upon a place to put your roses. Roses have several requirements if you want to have contented, healthy plants. Some people might scoff at my using the word "contented" about roses – but believe me, when you have an uncontented rose, you will certainly know.

First, roses need at least six hours of sunlight every day, or more if you can manage it. A few roses can take partial shade, such as 'Zephirine Drouhin' (1868), a nearly thornless climber with raspberry pink blossoms. (Zephirine is susceptible to powdery mildew and blackspot, but she's still a good pick.) Zephirine is a bit of a rarity in the rose world. Roses prefer full sun. The more shade a rose gets, the less it blooms, and the more leggy and unhealthy it will get.

One bonus on growing roses in full sun: On some varieties, sunlight enhances the leaves, adding a striking bronze or maroon color to the dark green leaves – a very handsome effect.

Second, roses prefer a spot with good drainage. They need a lush, well-drained soil that holds moisture, but they don't want a place where water puddles for long periods of time. If you have this kind of heavy soil or a low area in your yard, you might consider growing the roses in raised beds.

Third, roses generally will need an inch of water every week to keep blooming. In high summer when everything was dry, I'd leave the drip irrigation system going all day. Obviously I didn't have the water going full tilt – this was, after all, a soaker hose/drip irrigation system – but the irrigation system gave the roses a steady trickle right at the roots that soaked deeply into the soil. The roots will follow the water deep into the cool soil. This in turn helps protect the plant from drought.

Fourth, give roses a light soil rich in organic material. They do all right in clay soil, but they'll be much happier in a clay soil with compost, rotted manure, and peat moss, along with soil amendments such as bone and blood meal or greensand, and perlite to make the soil lighter. (More information on these and other organic soil amendments can be found on page 42.) When you prepare the planting site, lay your soil amendments over the top of the ground evenly where you want your roses to go, then till or dig them in.

Fifth, give your roses space. To do this, find out how wide your rose bush gets. Often the width on a rose bush is the same as the height, so if you have a shrub rose that gets four feet tall, then give it that much space when you plant it. Then add three feet between the edge of one rose and the edge of the next. Your roses need good air circulation between them to keep down diseases. Also, you should have space between your rose bushes so you can walk through your garden without getting shredded by thorns.

Be sure to put the roses where you can see and enjoy them, of course, some place where you feel you can stand and admire them and stick your nose in the blossoms without fear of censure. Bonus points if you can place them where the breeze wafts their fragrance through an open window into your house.

Finally, find a place where there's some air circulation, where the breeze moves through. This helps to keep the foliage dry and keeps diseases down. Now, if you live in an area with perpetual high winds, you might have to plant tougher roses. Rugosa roses are hardy and can take strong winds due to their thick, glossy foliage. Rugosas are often planted near the sea because salt spray doesn't faze them, either. But roses in windy locations will need more water due to the winds drying out leaves and especially their blossoms.

No place is perfect, but even imperfect planting sites can be fixed. In a low-lying place, a raised bed will get a rose's feet out of the water. A windy area can be protected by a screen of evergreens. A shady place can be brightened by removing some overhanging tree limbs. Sometimes a few small adjustments can fix many ills.

LAMARQUE (N). WHITE, SHADED LEMON, FLOWERS NATURALLY IN CLUSTERS.

'Lamarque' (1830), a cross between 'Blush Noisette' and 'Parks Yellow Tea-Scented China,' is a vigorous climber/rambler, very fragrant, and is available from the Antique Rose Emporium.

The Importance of Soil Building

In all my years of horticulturing, I am convinced that there's one thing that, done well, assures the success of your garden (besides simple maintenance, of course), and that is soil building. If your soil contains natural organic matter like compost, aged manure, or peat moss, and if it's mulched with leaves, straw, wood chips, or grass clippings that can decay into the soil – then you'll have healthy plants.

I've seen barren soil that has had no organic matter added to it in years. This soil is flat, gray, and hard to dig into because all the earthworms that could have been loosening the soil have died. Plants can grow in this soil, but only through the help of chemical fertilizers.

Truly healthy soil is far more than just dirt. Your soil, whether it's sandy, silty, loamy, clay, or something in between, is held together by a dynamic living system with complex physical and chemical properties – an amazing, invisible world beneath the soles of your feet. Your soil is teeming with microbes: Bacteria, algae, yeast, actinomycetes (a type of very beneficial bacteria), fungus – as well as larger creatures like earthworms, pillbugs, nematodes, and many more creatures. In a very fertile soil, the amount of bacteria in one acre can weigh up to *600 pounds*. These, too, enrich the soil when they die. There are untold numbers of these organisms working and living in your soil, making a complex ecological web in the soil and around your roses' roots. This unseen world is of the greatest benefit to your plants.

Fertile soil is also made up of pores. Earthworms make the soil porous by digging burrows through plant roots, or deep into the ground where they bring up subsoil and the nutrients locked within it to the soil's surface. Pores are also created by where plant roots have grown and then decayed. All these spaces in the soil help water to soak down deeply. Pores allow oxygen to reach plant roots and fuels the work of soil microbes, which break organic materials down into humus.

These days, gardeners are returning to a more natural "top-down" soil building regimen. In nature, soil fertility is generally accomplished through mulches (leaves falling on the forest floor; grasses and plants dying in fall), and through roots decaying in the ground. Digging isn't necessary in a natural system. So, for the gardener, this means less labor – which is always a good thing if you happen to have a bad back.

So be generous with your compost. Be generous with your mulches. Use leaves that you've chopped up with your lawnmower, grass clippings (only herbicide-free clippings), straw, bark, wood chips – any organic materials that break down into your soil. (I have more on composting and on organic fertilizers later in the book.)

Feed the soil, and feed the complex web of life under your feet. I guarantee that if you do this, you will see good results from your roses.

Rosa gallica – A rose dating back to the Middle Ages with a nice fragrance and purplish-red blossoms. When roses were considered too hedonistic for monastery gardens (thanks a lot, you hedonistic Romans), this rose was kept around due to its many medicinal properties.

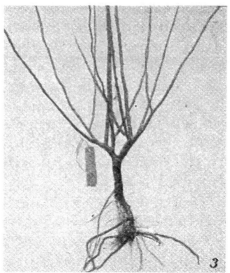

A bareroot rose.

SHOPPING FOR ROSES

How to Buy Bare-Root Roses

Have you ever seen a bare-root rose? When you pull one out of the cool, moist mulch it's stored in, all you see are a couple of thorny sticks on top, a couple of black roots on the bottom … if this *is* the bottom …. And you think, I'm spending twenty-some bucks for this? However, a good bare-root rose is worth every cent.

Bare-roots are much easier to handle than a big potted rose. (They're much easier to send through the mail, too, if you order them through a catalog.) The selection of bare-roots early in the year is far better than what you will get with the potted roses later. Also, bare-root roses give you a head start on the planting season. It doesn't matter how cold it is; bare-root roses can be planted as soon as the ground can be worked in early spring. Bare-root roses are dormant. Once you plant them, they "wake up" in their new home, and so they don't get transplant shock the way potted roses do.

Remember that the very things that make bare-root roses great for early-season planting also make them very vulnerable to heat, sun, and drying winds. For best results, plant them as early in the season as possible. If you can't avoid planting them late in the season, give them as much protection as possible through the process. (That is, bury them in mulch!)

Of course, before you purchase any rose, take time to make a good home for it. Choose a place with good, fertile soil that gets six or more hours of light daily. Avoid windy areas that will sap moisture from the leaves and canes. Keep the roses well away from trees, because roses are very heavy feeders, and the trees will steal nutrients from them.

Purchasing a bare-root rose.

Bare-root roses come in three grades – Grade 1, Grade 1.5, and Grade 2. The Grade 1 roses are of the highest quality. If you want to get *really* technical, Grade 1 roses have at least three strong canes, branched no higher than 3 inches above the bud graft, and each cane measures at least 5/16 inch in diameter. Grade 1.5 roses have only two canes. Grade 2 roses have one 5/16-inch cane and at least one at 1/4 inch. The Grade 1 roses are strongest and most vigorous.

When you inspect your bare-root rose, look for large (but tightly closed) buds and a reasonable number of large canes (at least three). Most bare-root roses will have green skin, but some will be brown. To check if the rose is alive, scratch away a bit of the rose's skin with your fingernail. The cambium layer underneath should be green if the rose is living.

If the rose has started growing, don't buy it. Bare-root roses do best if they're still dormant when you plant them. If the top of the rose starts growing before the rose's roots do, the rose can't pull water and nutrients out of the ground fast enough to support this new growth. (Imagine being very thirsty, but you have to drink your water through a straw that's as skinny as a coffee stirrer. That's what's happening to this poor rose.) Then it uses up its stored energy and dies.

Your best bet is to buy roses that are fully dormant, with tight buds and no growth.

Own-root roses and grafted roses.

There are two types of roses: Own-root roses and grafted roses. Grafted roses are where the rose canes are grafted onto a hardy set of roots (often a 'Dr. Huey' rose or a multiflora rose). They'll have a swollen area on the neck of the rose, between the canes and the roots – that's the graft union. Roses are grafted onto rootstocks because it takes a long, long time to grow rose cuttings on their own roots. Some roses, such as grandifloras, are fussbudgets and won't grow until they're stuck onto a hardy rootstock. But own-root roses are hardier and healthier – a better choice if you can get them.

The bare-root rose may need a little "cleaning up" when you get it. Wipe off any white mold you see. The roots should be cut back about a half-inch, and broken stems and roots should be trimmed off. At some nurseries, the rosarians will do this for you if you ask politely.

If you order your bare-root roses through the mail, open and inspect your order as soon as you get it. Tell your supplier if any of your roses are growing new shoots. These roses have broken dormancy, so if they fail in the garden and die, you should be able to get them replaced.

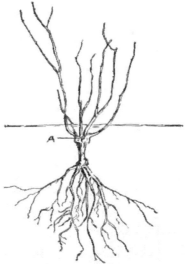

2176. A typical dormant Rose
as it should be planted.

In this diagram, "A" is the bud union. If the rose is grown on its own roots, "A" is just below where the branches meet the stem, and this can sit at soil level.

Planting bare-root roses

If you can't plant your roses immediately, put them in a container filled with moist peat moss. Be sure the roots are well-covered, and keep the container in a cool, shaded location.

You can also heel in your roses in a hole or trench in the ground.

If you're replacing a rose that has been planted in the same spot for over ten years, plant the rose elsewhere, or replace the soil before planting. Places that have grown roses for many years are prone to a malady called "sick soil."

Roses stop flourishing in that soil, mainly (it is thought) because pests and diseases have accumulated in the soil.

Also, if you have what I call "subdivision soil" – a dense, compacted soil created by heavy machinery churning up subsoil during construction – you will have to dig out all that lousy soil or create raised beds before you plant roses.

Now, prepare the soil. Be sure to get all the weeds out. Mark where you want the roses to go in, giving each rose three feet of space – and take into consideration how wide your rosebush will actually get!

Here is a nice, spacious hole for a bare-root rose. Be sure to dig a nice, spacious hole for container roses, too.

How to Dig a Hole

About 24 hours before you're ready to plant, fill a five-gallon bucket with water. Add a splash of bleach (1/8 cup to a five-gallon bucket) to the water to clean up any bacteria. Pour in a cup of root stimulant, and put your bare-root roses in. Let them sit in the water until you plant them.

Protip: Before you dig, lay a tarp down next to the hole. Put all your dug-up soil here. When you've finished planting your rose and used the excess soil to make a saucer around the rose, pick up the tarp – and the ground where you were digging is just as clean as can be.

While the rose is soaking in its bucket, prepare a great hole to plant the rose in. This part is very important, because a quality hole will grow a quality rose.

Dig a generous hole that's about two feet wide and 18 inches deep. Take out part of that soil, then mix in compost and peat moss (or other organic matter); add fertilizers such as Osmocote, bone meal, blood meal, or Bradfield – about a cup of any of these. Also, add soil amendments such as perlite, peat moss, well-rotted or composted manure, compost, kelp meal, greensand, or whatever good amendments you have available.

The soil amendments you add don't have to be scientifically balanced. Many times I simply use what I have at hand. "Well, here's a half-bale of peat moss, so I'll divide that among these six rose holes. Here's some Bradfield – let's give 'em a cup each. I have two buckets of compost from the landfill, we'll dump a little into each hole. Shoot, I have only two cups of bone meal for six roses, but I'm not going to waste half the morning running to the store. Split it up. Something's better than nothing. Okay, that looks good, let's grab the shovel and mix it all in with the soil in the holes. Maybe I'll even get this part of the job done by lunchtime." (Looks at watch.) "Or not."

What you want (technically, what your *plant* wants) is to have plenty of organic material, a light and crumbly soil, and plentiful nutrients. Nature is not scientifically precise about soil building, but she balances it all out in the end.

When you are ready to plant, take your roses out of the water they're soaking in, put them in a garbage sack to keep the roots from drying out, and bring them to the planting site. Also bring your shovel, your soil amendments, a tarp, and the garden hose.

Make a cone of soil in the middle of the hole. The cone should come up under the roots and support the rose.

Now, lay your shovel handle across the top of the hole – this will show you where soil level will be once the rose is planted. When you set your rose on the cone, the bud union of the rose – that big knob that connects the canes with the roots – should sit three to five inches below the shovel handle. Adjust the height of the cone until the bud union is the right height.

Fill in the rest of the soil and firm it around the bush. Use the extra soil to make a saucer around the rose – this saucer will keep the water and mulch from running off.

Gently build a mound of soil over the top six inches of the rose canes, or even higher to protect the rose canes from drying out. Once the weather warms up, you can wash away this soil a little at a time. Cut back the canes that are sticking out of the mulch so they don't pull moisture out of the rose.

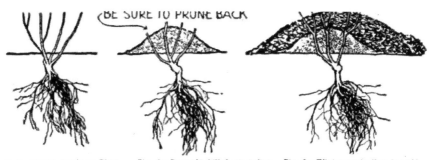

1) Proper depth to plant. 2) Properly hilled up after planting.
3) Winter protection in cold regions.

If you buy a rose that's had its canes dipped in wax, remember that the wax acts as an anti-desiccant, and keeps the canes from drying out when in transit, or when sitting around in a store waiting to be bought. Wax also good to have on the rose when the weather is too cold for foliage to grow. However, the wax needs to be off by March to allow the buds to grow. You can flake the wax off the end of the cane, or scrub it with a toothbrush (obviously, don't brush your teeth with this later). Or, you can simply pour warm water over the rose to melt off enough wax to help the rose along. Once you're done, cover the exposed canes in mulch or soil, or spray them with an anti-desiccant like Wilt-Pruf to keep valuable moisture from escaping.

Post-planting care.

When shoots start coming out of the mound of mulch, then start removing it, little by little. Don't remove all of the mulch, though. Leave a little extra on the rose through the first year to keep the tender roots well-shaded and to slow down water loss from the canes and new shoots during the hot summer. Next year, uncover the rose fully.

Once the shoots start growing, this rose will need to be fertilized monthly, and watered weekly. Fish emulsion is a good fertilizer – though every fly within a mile will stop by to see what that lovely fragrance is. A good brand of fish emulsion is Fish Bliss. Mix fish emulsion in a five-gallon bucket according to label instructions, then water the roses with it.

If a soil test shows that your soil is low in magnesium, then pour a ½ cup of Epsom salts around the rose to encourage basal breaks – these are where the new buds form on the bud union – so your rose will grow many new canes. (If you have trouble with too much salt in your soil, skip this step.)

Have at least two inches of mulch all over the rose bed to keep the weeds down, the ground cool, and the earthworms busy. The thing I really love about mulch is that earthworms will be working clear up to the surface of the soil where the mulch is. Even in February, I've moved the mulch aside and found worm castings on the surface of the ground – which is solid gold to plants. The nutrients in the worm castings are chelated – that is, they're in a form that is easy for the plants to take in. Chelated nutrients are like candy to a plant. Keep that in mind the next time you see earthworm castings.

Alfalfa meal (be sure it doesn't have any additives) is great for roses. As it breaks down, it yields a growth stimulant called triacontanol. The Organic Gardening Research Center found that small amounts of triacontanol increased vegetable yields by 30 to 60 percent. Alfalfa also contains trace minerals such as iron, potassium, and magnesium that enrich the soil. These nutrients and elements are slowly released to the plant, so they don't leach away after a rainstorm.

I used to give alfalfa meal to my roses, but when I switched over to Bradfield fertilizer, oh man, I could see the difference. I scattered a cup of Bradfield fertilizer around each rose in early May, and after I watered it in, the roses just popped with blossoms and they looked gorgeous. I was completely sold after that. Bradfield fertilizer, an all-natural fertilizer, contains alfalfa and other great substances that make your roses sit up and grow like crazy.

Two things about Bradfield fertilizer that you should remember. First, be sure to water it in when you apply it, so you can get all that good stuff down to the plant roots. Second, be sure animals aren't around when you put it down. Dogs, cats, and ducks like to eat it because of the molasses it contains. (The molasses feeds essential microbes in the soil to stimulate the soil biomass, thereby helping to create a healthier soil.) It's okay if animals eat the fertilizer, because it's non-toxic. Still, it's frustrating.

A number of ducks lived in the Krug Park lagoon. One spring I threw down some Bradfield around the roses. The ducks waddled over and dabbled through the mulch until they'd eaten it all. From then on, I dug the Bradfield into the ground. Those feathered jerks.

Giving bare-root roses a good start seems like a lot of fuss and bother. But next year, when these roses really start taking off, believe me, you will be so amazed at what those little thorny sticks can become.

These directions also apply to container roses. Don't pack the soil in with your feet, though – water it in to avoid compaction.

What To Look For In Container-Grown Roses

In spring, when the roses show up at the nurseries, it's easy to get all excited and just start grabbing roses like a kid in a candy store. Okay, I should probably speak for myself. At any rate, as you stroll through a greenhouse full of new roses, all blooming and looking gorgeous, here are a few tips to help you choose the best one.

For container roses, look for plants with lots of healthy canes; robust, glossy leaves; moist but not wet soil, unless they just finished their daily watering; and new canes that are really growing well with lots of leaves. Check for bugs and diseases on the leaves. Also, compare a rose to its neighbors to see if it looks healthier ... or decidedly unhealthy.

Look for robust roses with dark-green or bronze leaves (avoid roses with really pale leaves, or have a strange-looking veins that other leaves don't). A good rose has lots of strong stems and leaves that are shiny and healthy.

Sometimes at big retailers, you'll see roses that look sad, under watered, or the foliage looks odd. In these cases, you might go to a different place. Their roses might be cheap, but as with everything, you get what you pay for. Retailers are really bad about taking care of plants, often leaving them to wilt, or overwatering them. Retail stores are good for bargains, but if you want a high-quality plant and knowledgeable staff, start at your local nurseries.

If the rose is blooming, it's a good idea to take off the flowers before you plant it. Plants tend to direct all their energy toward blossoms, so they won't be working so hard on extremely important things – like making roots. It's okay to whimper a little when you are cutting off the blossoms. This will help the rose, I promise!

When you choose the location and dig the hole for the potted rose, follow the instructions I laid out in the chapter for bare-root roses. However, for a potted rose, you'll dig the hole a little deeper to fit the whole rootball in.

As before, lay your shovel handle flush on the ground so you can gauge where soil level is. Set your potted plant into the hole to see if it fits, and keep digging if necessary.

This next part is important. You need to check where the bud union is on the rose so you can be sure it will be planted deep enough to be safe against the cold (again, three to five inches deep). With your fingertips, gently dig the soil away from the stem until you find the big bump where the bud union is. (If the bud union is clearly visible, the digging will not be necessary.) With the bud union visible, readjust the depth of your pot.

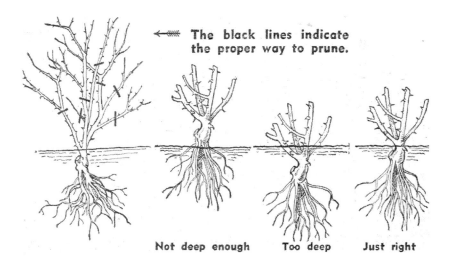

The black lines indicate the proper way to prune.

Not deep enough   Too deep   Just right

Taking the rose out of the pot can be problematic sometimes. If your potted rose is too young to have put out many roots, the soil might crumble as you take it out. Conversely, if you're planting this rose late in the season, you might get a rootbound plant – which simply means that the roots have circled upon themselves inside the pot. If there are roots coming out of the drainage hole, then your plant is definitely rootbound.

Here's a good way to get it out of the pot. Lay the pot down on its side, with the plant sticking out over the hole you've dug for it. If the rose is badly rootbound, thump around the outside of the pot to help release the soil and roots. Put your strongest hand around the rose stem. Pick up the pot with your other arm and gently tip it forward so your strong hand can gently pull the rose out of the pot. Slide the pot off with your other hand, then grab the rootball and set the plant into the hole.

You can even slide the rootball into the hole onto its side, and then set it upright.

Check one more time to see that the bud union is deep enough, and adjust the rootball if necessary. Scoop in the best soil around the lowest roots, fill in the hole, then make a nice saucer around the rose.

For the first watering, I generally have a five-gallon bucket standing by with some fish emulsion (Fish Bliss) or Miracle-Gro, and water the rose with that to give her a good start. When you water, see how well the saucer you made holds the water, and fix any leaks you see in your miniature levee.

When you are done watering, give your rose a nice, deep layer of mulch. Congratulations, you're done!

The 'Duchess of Albany' rose, a dark red rose which was a sport of 'La France,' no longer seems to be in commerce.

Buying and Planting Roses in the Fall

It happens every year: After being blasted by summer heat for months and months, I step outside with the bulldog one morning to find the air suddenly, unseasonably cool. And something about the coolness of the air makes me realize that yes, it is September: Apple season, the month of turning maples, and the warm scent of fallen leaves.

Fall is a great time of year to plant. Perennials, shrubs, trees, and especially roses – all these benefit from fall planting. Fall planting gives the roses fall, winter, and spring to become established before they are broiled in the summer sun. Planting in the cool of fall, when the evaporation rate is low, keeps the rose from drying out and wilting. This allows the plant to use its energy to send its roots deep.

Even if the roses aren't fully established by the time winter hits, the roots in the soil are at least "heeled in" -- that is, protected from the severest bite of winter cold. Roots will also grow during the winter. Though it's deucedly hard for biologists to study roots, especially in winter conditions, research indicates that roots act quite independently of the upper part of the plant. During very cold conditions, roots fall dormant. However, when the ground is insulated from extremely cold temperatures – whether by a thick layer of snow or by mulch – the roots will absorb water and nutrients, repair themselves, and grow. This quiet underground activity yields great dividends for the plant in spring.

Potted roses are on sale in the fall. Selection will be limited, and some of the roses might look bedraggled because they've been stuck in a pot since April. However, this is still a good time to browse, because you never know what you'll find. And, because the roses are on sale, you can grab one that looks a little ragged, or something you might not have ordinarily grown, just to see how it turns out. If it doesn't turn out, well, you didn't spend very much money on it anyway. And if the rose hits the jackpot, well, then, you can tell everyone that this rose was one of the best bargains you ever found!

How to Transplant a Rose

Maybe you're moving, or you're trying to rescue a rose from a construction site, or you've found a lovely antique rose on an abandoned homestead and have gotten the landowner's permission to move it. Here are some steps to help you transplant these beauties.

The best time to transplant is in late fall, because this allows the rose to recover somewhat before new growth starts in spring. Sometimes, though, you can't afford to wait. You can move a rose at any time of year, when it comes down to it.

The first step is actually very important: Figure out where in your yard you want the transplanted rose to go. Then dig the hole where your rose is going to go!

Why dig the hole first? Because by the time you wrestle a gigantic rose out of the ground, hoist it into your truck, and get it back home, you are going to be tired. So if you have the hole ready with a five-gallon bucket of fish emulsion or Miracle-Gro sitting there ready to go, all you have to do is dump the rose into the hole, cover it up, water it in, and then lie down on the lawn and take a well-deserved nap. For the win!

Dig a spacious hole that will be big enough to accommodate the rose's rootball, and deep enough to keep the bud union (if it has one) three to five inches underground. I have the full overview on page 20 in "How to Dig a Hole."

Once your planting site is ready to receive your rose, NOW you can go over and dig it up. Sorry to have kept you waiting. Believe me, you'll thank me when you're done.

Before you dig the rose up, prune it to make the move easier. Cut out deadwood and the oldest, thickest canes. Cut out slender twigs and crossed canes. Once you've cleaned up the rose bush, cut it back by a third, or even a half.

Have a wet sheet or piece of burlap ready for the next part of the operation: Digging up the rose. Use a sharp spade to cut the ground all around the rootball, then cut underneath the rootball. If the spade isn't sharp enough, you'll have to go in with pruning shears or limb cutters to sever the largest roots. Once the rootball is loose in the hole, lean it away from you and slide the wet burlap or sheet into the ground under and around it. Tip the rose the other way so it's lying on the sheet, and pull the sheet the rest of the way under the rootball. Once you've gotten the sheet all the way under the rootball, knot it, then use the sheet or burlap to lift it out of the ground.

If you have to transport the rootball any distance, wrap the sheet in a garbage bag to keep moisture in. (Wrap the whole rose if it is small enough.)

Once you get the rose to your planting site, measure the rose's rootball, then measure the hole to make sure that the bud union will be three to five inches underground once you put the rootball in. Adjust the hole if needed, then set the rose in. Lean it first one way to slide the sheet under it, then lean it the other way to wriggle the sheet out. Set the rose upright, backfill, make a saucer around the rose, pour in that five-gallon bucket of water, water it in with the hose, and put on a heavy layer of mulch.

You're done!

Be sure to give the new rose a good drink every week, unless you get over an inch of rain.

CARING FOR ROSES

Watering: Give Roses a Good Long Drink

When you first plant roses, water them with 5 to 10 gallons of water. Use a 2-gallon watering can or a 5-gallon bucket and water s-l-o-w-l-y. Slow pour, not fast splash.

The best way to water a rose is to give it a good long soak. Eudora Welty said that her mother always remembered the classic advice to rose growers on how to water their roses long enough: "Take a chair and *St. Elmo*." (This popular Southern novel is pretty long but certainly worth a read, especially if you love flowery antebellum romance.) If you have a sprinkler or a soaker hose, let it run over the garden for several hours. If you water with a shower wand, take it slow, and don't use the mist setting. Looks are deceiving: When the foliage and mulch look wet, one may think it's time to stop watering. However, if you take a trowel and dig into the soil, the water has hardly penetrated the surface. (A lot of recent showers have watered the land in this way, leaving the subsoil like a brick.) By watering deeply, you encourage roots to sink deep. Shallow watering leaves roots near the soil surface, where heat can burn them.

Newly planted roses need extra water. Roses need an inch of water weekly, and these days, the water simply ain't coming from the sky. Let the garden hose trickle on the rose for an hour or so. Let it run just enough to form a puddle on the ground, but not so fast that you end up with a mire over half the yard. Also, place a reminder somewhere (I have found sticky-notes on the forehead to be effective) to shut the water off before you go to sleep.

However, don't go overboard and water every day! Too much water can do as much harm as too little, especially in shady and protected gardens that don't need as much water.

If you're watering in the evening, keep the leaves dry, since sometime water on the leaves overnight will bring on diseases faster. However, if the day's bright, hot, and sunny, spray the leaves to your heart's content; it'll dry. This is a good way to discourage spider mites, too, since they hate cool and moist conditions.

HYBRID PERPETUAL ROSE, GLOIRE LYONAISE. 25 CTS.

'Gloire Lyonnaise' (about 1885) is a repeat-blooming ivory-white rose, strongly fragrant, with shiny dark green foliage.

Mulching: Saving Roots and Plants for Millennia

Once, during a scorching hot day, I was dragging the hose across the yard while the water was running. I noticed what I thought was a puff of dust rising from a barren spot in the lawn. When I looked closer, I realized that it wasn't dust at all, but *steam* from where the water splashed on the burning-hot soil. This is why mulch is so important to soil health.

In nature, trees and grasses will mulch the ground around plants. When you kick through the fallen leaves of the forest, you can dig down to where the decaying leaves have turned the soil rich and black with organic matter, and the forest soil is always cool and moist under the leaves. The same principles apply to your garden soil.

A two-inch layer of mulch protects the rose roots from that kind of heat. There's no substitute for mulch. It keeps the ground cool, keeps water from evaporating so quickly (so you can water less!), keeps mud from splashing on the plant leaves when you water, and, over time, adds needed organic material to the soil. I like wood chips or cypress mulch in the flower bed for that cultivated look (but not the red-dyed mulches – those are too garish). Grass clippings are good in the vegetable garden where you're going to be tromping around looking for ripe tomatoes. Why send grass and leaves to the landfill when they can play such an excellent part in mulching the soil? (And you can save money on fertilizer – money that you then blow on a bunch of antique roses. Priorities, you know.)

A BRANCH OF DUNDEE RAMBLER.

'Dundee Rambler,' (either 1850 or 1837), a rambling rose that gets up to 25' tall (or more – it's pretty vigorous). It bears loads of small white blooms with a myrrh fragrance. Blooms once a year.

Fertilizing: Feed the Rose and Feed the Soil

A rose that has a good fertilization regimen will bless you with blossoms upon blossoms even through the worst heat, as well as with glossy, healthy foliage.

So what exactly is a "good fertilization regimen?" Well, think of it as a balanced diet. For humans, a balanced diet consists of a variety of healthy foods from all four food groups. For roses, as with humans, your best results come with variety.

A good way to start your roses off in the early spring, before the leaves come out, is to apply compost or rotted manure around the rose. Compost reinvigorates the microorganisms in the soil while releasing nutrients slowly to the roses. For a real spring tonic, make a mixture of alfalfa meal, cottonseed meal, fish meal, and blood meal, and add a cup or two of this to your compost. Scratch all of this together into the soil around your roses, then cover it with a nice two-inch layer of mulch and water it in. These organic fertilizers will give your plant energy to gear up and start growing.

Avoid nitrogen fertilizers this early in the year, though. Nitrogen makes your rose grow soft, tender leaves – which turn black during a freeze. This time of year, slow leaf growth is best.

In late April or early May, it's time to give the rose a new fertilizer. My favorite organic fertilizer for this time of year is Bradfield Organics Natural Fertilizer. One of its main ingredients is alfalfa, which contains a natural growth stimulant that really makes the roses sit up and grow. Other ingredients include sulfate of potash, which is a low-salt, non-acidic form of potassium and sulfur; and humate, which is a soil conditioner that improves nutrient uptake in the plants and fights soil compaction. Use two cups of Bradfield per rosebush. Ideally, you'd scrape the mulch aside, scatter the fertilizer, scratch it into the soil, then cover it back up with the mulch – otherwise this fertilizer (due to the alfalfa in it) will mat and shed water in the rain. I had to bury this fertilizer because the danged ducks loved eating it. Either way, it still worked great.

Also, as soon as the first reddish/burgundy new growth stretches out its leaves, give the roses a foliar feeding with a chemical fertilizer like Miracle-Gro to feed your roses and supply micronutrients. If you start your spraying regimen early, you have better success with disease resistance down the line.

In May and June, when I got a moment, I'd also use fish emulsion as a super-quick source of nitrogen, phosphate, and potash. Fish emulsion is more of a tonic for the roses and the soil organisms – a short-term, not long-term, fertilizer. The roses love it, though.

Be warned that when you mix it, all the flies and cats and dogs in the neighborhood will show up, and some raccoons might mosey over to see where the catfish party is. So keep an eye on things if you have trouble with critters.

In these cases, give each rose about a gallon of fish emulsion, then rinse it into the soil with a water wand. The smell will go away, and so will all your new friends.

Also, give roses the gift of compost. In May, my daughter and I visited the Henry Doorly Zoo in Omaha, and we got a noseful of the manure they'd put on the roses in the Garden of the Senses. (How appropriate.) But you know those roses are going to reward those groundskeepers in June, and you know that nobody will notice the manure smell then! Composted manure is better for roses, though. It enriches the soil, and the earthworms love it. The more worms in the garden, the healthier the soil is.

Whatever fertilizer you use, the roses should be fertilized at least twice in May, then once a month from then on until September. I generally would give each rose a cup of Bradfield every month and a foliar feeding (fish emulsion, Miracle-Gro, or something) every month.

Be sure the fertilizer is low in nitrogen (N) and high in phosphorus (P) and potassium (K). Nitrogen greens up the foliage, but too much nitrogen makes the foliage soft and succulent – which bugs love. Phosphorus and potassium nourish roots, stems, and blossoms – a better deal overall for the rose, and for you.

A quick note: If you are a casual rose grower, fertilizing your roses once a month is fine. If you are a rose junkie growing exhibition-quality blooms, you can fertilize weekly – but cut the concentration of the fertilizer by half, or use half as much granular fertilizer.

MADAME FALCOT (T.), DEEP APRICOT, DERIVED FROM SAFRANO.

'Madame Falcot' (1853) is a vigorous hybrid tea with fragrant apricot blossoms, still available.

Compost Basics

Gardeners are so gung-ho over compost. (But, 'tis true, they have good reason.) At the end of every *Organic Gardening* magazine (before they decided to change their name and go to that all-picture format) was the feature "Compost Corner," where readers write stories about their compost heaps. And what stories! There's a fellow who has seven compost heaps smoking in the morning sun (and it's still not enough); there's a lady who is "quite sentimental" about her heap, the bin of which was constructed with the trunk of a Christmas tree.

When I took care of the rose garden, I could go to the city

landfill and they'd fill up my truck with compost. They made their compost from all that discarded yard waste people would bring in. The compost was messy, and I often found bits of plastic bags in it, but it was still great for the soil.

All that organic material improves the soil structure. Soil bacteria feed on the compost, producing starches that hold soil grains together; fungi also feed on it, and send out "threads" (in scientific talk, hyphae).

When you are gathering materials to build a compost pile, *Organic Gardening* states that a third of the compost should consist of fresh green materials like clippings, weeds and kitchen wastes. Another third should include "dead brown materials" like straw or leaves; and the last third should be of unfinished compost or soil, to provide micro-organisms that will get busy breaking down materials. (Don't worry if you don't have the right proportions; the stuff still breaks down just fine, but it might take a little longer.)

Manure is the best "green" material to add to your compost pile. It's filled with active microorganisms that will quickly heat your pile up, and is packed with energy that will activate your compost and make it hot. Definitely remember the rule of threes when adding the manure – add an equal amount of "brown" materials, and mix them very well. The brown materials will keep the manure from smelling. The final third is the soil or unfinished compost. Then you have a good balance between all three.

Keep the pile moist by watering it if it doesn't rain. Finally, turn the pile every couple of days. If the pile is fairly large, you might get a piece of rebar -- a metal rod used for reinforcing concrete -- or long pipe with which you can stir the pile. It's crucial to get air to the middle of the pile. The bacteria need oxygen to keep the pile hot.

The pile should get hot if it's composting well -- or "cooking." Don't leave your hand on the pipe, because compost that's really cooking can get quite hot. Some people actually wrap the pipe in duct tape to protect their hands.

Some researchers now say that you don't have to turn or stir if you mix in enough coarse material, like straw, when you build the pile. If this appeals to you, then experiment and see what happens. A big part of gardening is experimenting. Sometimes things work and sometimes they don't work. Then you figure out why it worked (or didn't) and try a different approach next time.

To be sure compost is well-done, put a little in a closed baggie for several days, then open it and take a whiff. Well-done compost will have an earthy scent. Then pour the compost over a screen to keep out huge clods, and take it out into the garden. They call it black gold, and you will too, when you see the difference in your plants.

Chickens: They're fun and they also provide fertilizer!

Great Organic Fertilizers for Roses

Every rosarian wants to have huge, healthy roses. One of the keys to this is to properly care for and feed the soil.

Chemical fertilizers such as Miracle-Gro certainly nourish your roses with minerals and nutrients. However, they don't add anything to the soil. Chemical fertilizers are like multivitamins: They do you good, but in the long run, it's best to eat a balanced diet. In terms of soil health, the "balanced diet" comes from feeding the soil. When you add plenty of organic material to the soil, you start a process that works for both the soil and the plants that grow in it.

Microorganisms break the organic material down, making the soil looser and more crumbly. Earthworms further break the organic material down, then expel it in the form of worm castings. If you've ever seen how plant roots wrap around worm burrows, you've seen for yourself how much plants love the nutrients that worms make available in the soil. Also, the burrows bring air deep into the ground and ease soil compaction, which is also good for roots.

But there are many other organic ingredients that you can add to the soil to improve it, as well as stimulants to boost growth in your roses.

This is not a comprehensive list by any means, but any of these will be helpful in your rose garden. You can rotate fertilizers, change one out for another over the year. Or if your local nursery runs out of one fertilizer, you can grab another of these off the list and still be fine.

Greensand – This is an organic soil amendment that you don't hear a lot about, but it's great for soil. It's a material called glauconite, mined from where the ocean floor used to be (i.e. New Jersey), and contains many of the nutrients and minerals you'd find in seawater (except salt). It's an especially good source of potash (which stimulates photosynthesis in plants), and also silica, magnesia, iron oxide, lime and phosphoric acid, and 22 trace minerals. It's a slow-release fertilizer (0-0-3) but it's a great conditioner for clay soils, improving its texture and loosening it up nicely. It also helps sandy soil retain moisture. Greensand absorbs and holds water very well. Apply this at about a quarter-pound per square foot of soil, or 50 to 100 pounds per 1,000 square feet. You can dig it into the soil when planting your roses, or broadcast it over the top of the soil, or even add it to your compost to enrich it.

Blood or bone meal – This is dried, powdered blood from slaughterhouses that's high in nitrogen and iron. This should be added to the soil and dug in, because if you use this as a top-dressing (i.e. sprinkle it on top of the soil), dogs and cats and critters will be nosing around and licking your mulch.

Blood meal is supposed to keep rabbits away. I think it's because all these dogs and cats come into your yard to investigate that delicious smell. Till it in when using, or water it in to keep your dog friends away.

Manure – Manure is generally low in minerals, but it's one of the best soil conditioners, adding much-needed organic matter to the ground that breaks down very nicely to humus, which plants love. But, more important, manure is a biologically-active material, busy with microorganisms and bacteria that are the powerhouses that keep your soil busy and alive.

Fish emulsion – The cats will come running when you start watering your plants with this! But it's an excellent source of nitrogen and the plants love it. Roses especially. Fish Bliss is a nice brand.

Fish bits – If you've been fishing and have finished filleting your fish, take the stinky parts and bury them in the garden and water them in. Then you'll grow a fish tree!

No, actually, fish bits are great for plants. It's said that when the Seneca planted corn, they put a fish in the soil by every plant. It works for roses, too. But water after planting your fish so you wash away the fish smell and the animals don't dig it up. (If you *do* get a fish tree, please give me a call.)

Epsom salts – The magnesium in this stops blossom-end rot in tomatoes and helps roses to grow new canes. Put a half-cup around each plant once a year. However, if you have a high-salinity soil with too much salt in it, skip this step.

Tea and coffee grounds – These contain nitrogen, and make super mulch for acid-loving plants. They seem to stimulate growth in some plants, too. I watered my orchids with a little coffee added to a cup of water, and they greened up nicely. The caffeine acts as a stimulant for them too. They probably won't need a pot every morning, though, thanks.

Cottonseed meal – Good for adding nitrogen. This by-product from cotton manufacturing is good for acid-loving plants, which includes roses. I tried it as a mulch but was unimpressed, as it tended to repel water. Generally when I'd put this down, I'd lay some wood chips on top to help keep it moist. This might work better as a soil amendment and as a top-dressing for plants (one cup per rose).

Kelp and seaweed fertilizers – Kelp fertilizers can be applied as a granular fertilizer, or used as a foliar fertilizer that can be sprayed on the leaves. Kelp contains many trace nutrients, and may possibly contain small amounts of growth stimulants that will give you lush foliage and richly-colored blossoms. Seaweed sprays, on the other hand, can be sprayed as a foliar feed once a month, and might possibly help your leaves become more resistant to fungal diseases (blackspot and powdery mildew).

VISCOUNTESS FOLKESTONE (H.T.) A BEAUTIFUL ROSE FOR MASSING IN BEDS.

'Viscountess Folkestone' (1886), a robust, graceful rose with creamy pink blossoms with a fine fragrance. A favorite of some really, really old rosarians.

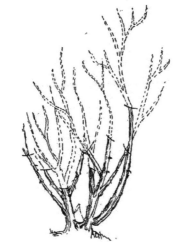

Suggestions on how to prune a rose.

PRUNING AND TRAINING

Deadheading

One afternoon I grabbed my pruners and called to my husband, "Honey, I'm going outside to deadhead the roses."

"What do roses have to do with the Grateful Dead?"

Boooo! A punster! Get him off the stage!

Deadheading is when you take the old flowers off the plant before they set seed. The whole meaning of life to a plant (as far as we know, that is) is to produce seed so a new generation of plants will grow after the mother plant dies. When you remove faded and spent flowers before they set seed, the plant turns its energy toward producing more flowers.

When you cut off a finished blossom, make your cut above the first five-leafed leaflet. Repeat-blooming roses should be cut back to wood that's strong enough to support a new rose.

Once in a while, you'll find that the first five-leafleted leaf is way, way, way down the stem. In this case, I move back up the stem, looking for a bud that's opening up and leafing out. Then I cut above that, angling the cut away from the bud. When you cut down to the leaf that's sprouting, you give the rose a good bud to start growing on, and blooming on, later.

On the once-blooming antique roses, you can remove the flowers without cutting clear back, because once blooming is finished, you will be cutting the whole bush back anyway.

Deadheading won't give you instant blooms, of course. Give the roses a little time to make new flowers. Some will reward you with continuing blooms, while some roses will wait until autumn to reward you. Whatever makes the rose happy is the best thing to do.

A Quick Primer in Making a Good Cut

1) This cut is too high above the bud.
2) See how ragged that cut is? This is bad for the plant.
3) This cut is too close to the bud.
The best cut would be a little bit above the bud, sloping away from it.

Rose Tips Through the Year

'Clotilde Soupert' (1890) has blush-pink blossoms, crazy climbing rose vigor, nearly thornless canes, ability to take shade, and she covers herself with highly-fragrant flowers.

Rose Tips for High Summer

Another name for beauty is rose. What other gift is wrapped so tightly as a rosebud but is so generous in its opening? What other fragrance is as sweet, even in the crushed leaves and stems of the shrub?

But, boy, those thorns sticking in your flesh can make you cuss like the devil.

When roses meet the summer heat, they swoon. Help them through this season with these tips.

Roses need deadheading. Dead or dying blooms should be removed to encourage new growth and the formation of new blooms. Use a pair of sharp clippers to cut the blossom off just above the first leaf with five leaflets on it. If that five-leafletted leaf is way way down the stem, just find the first new bud that's sprouting under the blossom, and cut just above that. The cut should slope away from the bud at about a 45-degree angle so rain or moisture doesn't collect there. Now, some have a little Elmer's multipurpose glue handy, and seal these cuts with a little cap of glue in order to keep the rose cane borers from tunneling into your rose cane through the cut. (Rose cane borers, which are small wasps, will go to the soft pith exposed by your cut and dig straight down into your rose stem to build nests for their young.) I never used the glue (I seldom had the time!), and naturally I had rose borers digging into my roses all the time. Charles over at Moffet's Nursery swears by the Elmer glue method, so you should probably listen to him.

ROSA RUGOSA.

Be sure to get the multipurpose glue, because school glue will wash off in the rain, leaving your cane open to the wasps.

I'm a little rougher with the rugosa roses. These roses have so many blossoms that I don't have time to clip every little stem. I just pull the hips off the rose bush and throw them back into the rose! (This time of year, I'm using every shortcut I can, in order to stay ahead of the weeds and the thousand other jobs a horticulturist is heir to.)

The stems on the dead rugosa blossoms are easily broken, and the roses are tough enough to take this kind of rough treatment.

Sterilize your clippers between roses to keep from spreading diseases, such as the dreaded rose rosette virus, from one plant to the next. (You can read more about rose rosette virus on page 84.) I use a 1:6 solution of bleach to water, measuring out a capful of bleach and six capfuls of water into my little bucket. Then I put a small cloth in there. Between roses, I clean both the anvil blade and cutting blade with the cloth, rubbing well.

Blackspot and powdery mildew will take their toll on roses this time of year, especially if a rainy spring has kept you from spraying on schedule. Pick off badly-diseased leaves to keep the spores from infecting new growth, then spray the roses with a systemic fungicide. Systemic fungicides, which are sprinkled into the ground around the rose (always read and follow label directions) seem to work more reliably than those that need to be reapplied after every rain. Also, I can skip a week with systemics and not have too much trouble. But a fungicide must be sprayed regularly. Otherwise, in July most roses will turn into blackspot on a stick.

Studies in Britain concluded that a 50/50 mix of skim milk and water stopped fungal diseases. Interesting! So if you have some milk that's close to expiration date, mix it with water and spray it on your roses.

Finally, fertilize the roses if you haven't already this

month. Whatever fertilizer you use, try to get it to them every other week. It's not going to have much effect during high summer, when roses go into a kind of dormancy. But it will yield great results in September, when the weather cools down a little and the roses pop back into glorious bloom.

Pile the mulch high over your roses' roots. I have seen sad little roses perk up once I covered their roots with a nice, thick layer of mulch. It was really gratifying.

Finally, be sure to water the roses deeply at least once a week, even twice a week if conditions are really hot and dry. I will spray the foliage with water during the heat of the day to give them a little relief.

COPYRIGHTED 1894
BY B. McGREGOR

BRIDESMAID.

November Rose Care

Early mornings are the best. (Once you wake up, that is.) A fall morning with roses is even better, despite cold fingers and nose.

I've come out to clip the leaves and buds off the roses. I hate to take the buds off, since the roses have been blooming all over. However, they need to prepare for winter, not expend energy in blooms that will be blasted by frost. The leaves have to go, too, so diseases and bugs on them are out of the garden for good.

I start work on the 'Zephirine Drouhin' climbers. I like working with these roses because they are thornless. Ladybugs are huddled between the newest leaves to shelter themselves from the cold. Once in a while, as I prune, the cane will bounce and the bug is catapulted into the air. "Sorry!" I cry.

Safrano.

When all the rose canes are bare, I take out any skinny or short canes, leaving only healthy, large canes. Then I'll spray them and the ground around them either with a copper fungicide, Mancozeb, or Maneb, on a warm afternoon. After the ground freezes, I'll mulch them.

It is quiet in the garden. A little junco, the first I've seen this year, hops through the leaves, then takes off. Chickadees whistle; nuthatches say "nah, nah" in soft voices.

By lunchtime, my coat is off. The ladybugs become industrious. They scurry up canes and when they get to the top, they open their popcorn-shell wings and zoom off. They know there's not much time before the real cold hits.

The honeybees, too, are all business. They don't particularly like the fact that I've been snipping blossoms.

"What's going on here?" they demand, hovering inches from my nose. I scoot back and take a short run, and they fly on to new business.

Thought fades into the rhythm of the clippers. It's hard to be businesslike, especially when "Folsom Prison Blues" is drifting through my head for the 1,285,386th time. "I hang my head down and cry." I guess it beats hearing the Raisin Bran jingle over and over.

But there's another song I'm hearing as maple leaves drift by in a glory of sunset colors. *Summer days are gone,* they say. *Summer days are gone.*

'Paul Neyron' (1869) bears gigantic dark pink blossoms full of petals. It's not very fragrant but it makes a tidy little shrub.

Winterize Your Roses

Don't be daunted by all the chores that must be done in the rose garden. Remember, it's okay if you don't do everything on the list. If you do just a few of the chores, the roses will bless you. Rose care is a limitless task, but don't knock yourself out over it.

In late fall, before the ground freezes, tuck in your roses for their long winter's nap.

Start by pruning your roses. Prune out small canes – those no thicker than a pencil – as well as canes that aren't tall enough to flower, damaged canes, canes that crisscross, or canes that are growing too close together. I leave anywhere from five to eight good canes on the rose for next year.

Then get rid of all the leaves you can. Leaves harbor diseases like blackspot and powdery mildew, as well as the eggs of insect pests. Clip the leaves off the rose and get them out of the garden. Use a leaf blower to clean up underneath the shrubs. Burn these leaves; don't put them on the compost pile.

If the soil is dry, give the roses a good drink of water. If the weather stays dry, water them every other week until the ground freezes.

Spray the roses and the ground around them with Maneb, Mancozeb, or copper fungicide to clean up any fungal diseases. You might even spray the roses with one of these fungicides a few times during the winter. I was reading an on-line study that hypothesized that winter sprayings help the rose defend itself against blackspot through the rest of the year. You might experiment and see if it works for you.

Now you're ready to cover the canes. You have several options.

Styrofoam cones. To use these, you cut your canes back just enough to fit the cone over the top of the rose, scrinch the cone over the shrub ("scrinch" is the hair-raising sound the canes make on the Styrofoam), find some way to anchor the cone to the ground so winter gales won't carry it away, and punch a few small holes in the sides to keep the temperatures inside the cone from getting too warm. Nothing easier!

Personally, I don't use these, partly because I'm cheap, but also because I don't cut back my roses as far as some rosarians do. (Technically, I hardly cut them back at all.) Styrofoam cones are best for hybrid teas that you cut back every year. Also, hybrid tea roses generally need the extra insulation.

Soil or compost. Mound about 12 inches of soil or compost over the rose. Do this gently, because a shovelful of soil, falling at the right angle, will snap the canes. (Get the soil from some other part of your garden so you don't disturb the rose roots.) Or use compost, which will be a valuable addition to next year's soil-building program. Some argue that soil or compost keep too much water around the stems, leading to rot. If you live in a part of the country where moisture and rot is a problem, you might try something else. Missouri, for our part, generally stays on the dry side, so we should have no problem with this.

Plain old mulch. Scoop it over the rose in a pile – again, carefully, to avoid breaking canes. When you uncover the rose in the spring, all you have to do is spread it out around the rose, and viola! You are done mulching the roses. Mulch doesn't keep the rose as well-protected as dirt, but (in my view) if a rose can't take the cold, it can go away and wilt. Final note: Mice might make nests in the mulch (though this has not been a problem for me).

Peat moss. This is a little more expensive, and you will have to wet it down before you put it on. By wetting it down, I mean you will have to reach in with your hands and rub the peat moss to make it soak up the water. Or you could split the bale and slowly run water into it until the peat moss absorbs the water. Or, you can go the careless route and leave the bale outside for several months with a couple of holes punched in it. By fall, the bale has absorbed the rain and is perfectly moist (and much heavier!) and ready to work. Be careful about breathing peat moss dust, because it's just annoying stuff. When I worked in a greenhouse, peat moss from the soilless mix would always be blowing around, and every time I blew my nose I'd have little peat moss specks in the Kleenex. I know, I know, too much information, but it's true.

Don't worry about choosing the best method. The best method is, inevitably, the one that's the least headache for you. However you cover them, the roses should be fine. If they do wimp out and die, get a tougher rose next year.

Every one of Them a
. . .Sparkler. . .

has been a favorite in all gardens where good yello
are planted for the past twenty years. There are 1

SOLVING ROSE-GROWING PROBLEMS

Fungicides – Because an Ounce of Prevention etc. etc.

I always tried to avoid growing plants with built-in health problems – my motto as horticulturist was, "If a plant can't take care of itself, then it can go away and wilt." On the other hand, some roses might have special significance for you, even though the poor dears get all racked with blackspot or powdery mildew in June. I have a rose, propagated via cuttings that my Great-great-great Grandma Chilcote was said to have grown, that turns white with powdery mildew every June – but I wouldn't give her up for anything. That's the way it goes.

The best way to beat fungal diseases is through preventative spraying. The best time to start is as soon as your rose starts growing its foliage in early spring.

Before I go further, I'm going to pause here and say that the very best way to keep disease down is to focus on the plant's health. Part of the reason that a rose develops diseases is that it's stressed in some way. It's the same with us – when everything is off-the-charts busy, and we're stressed, it seems like that is ALWAYS the time we catch the flu! Roses are the same way.

See that your rose getting enough water, add some compost to the soil, put mulch on the roots, and give it a fertilizer with all the major elements as well as all the micronutrients that are necessary for its health. If you work on your garden with your eye on always improving plant and soil health – that is, by using a plant-positive approach – diseases and insect outbreaks become easier to manage.

A Quick Guide to Blackspot and Mildew

Blackspot, powdery mildew, and downy mildew are diseases that preventative spraying can keep at bay.

Blackspot is a fungal disease that doesn't kill the rosebush but can cause it to lose leaves, further stressing the plant and leaving it more susceptible to more diseases. Blackspot starts when leaves develop small black spots, which get larger and spread to other leaves. Leaves will fall off the plant, and in severe cases the rose will be mostly defoliated. When treated, the spots will not go away, but new foliage will be clean of these spots.

Powdery mildew, also a fungal disease, starts as a small powdery-looking white spot on a leaf or stem, eventually spreading the white across the whole surface. Badly infected leaves will crumple slightly at the edges and along the veins. Powdery mildew is caused by poor air circulation when we have warm days and cool, wet nights. The spores of this fungus settle on rose leaves, stems, and buds. Roses that are not getting enough sunlight, and those that have been given too much nitrogen are susceptible to this disease.

Downy mildew is poorly named, because it doesn't look like a mildew, and it isn't even a fungus. Downy mildew is actually caused by an oomycete – a microorganism more closely related to brown algae than fungi. Downy mildew looks a lot like blackspot. Both diseases makes dark blotches on the leaves, but the difference is that blackspot makes round spots, while downy mildew makes purplish-black blotches that spreads from the veins across the leaves as well as your stems. It very, very quickly defoliates your plant, often within three days.

Downy mildew generally strikes when the weather is cool (55 to 65 degrees F) and the humidity is high (over 85 percent). (This is actually true of many fungal diseases.)

Other fungal diseases include **rust** (red spots appear on leaves; a mass of red spores is sometimes present) and **botrytis blight** (fuzzy gray mold grows on leaves or blossoms).

A preventative spraying program

It is important to start a weekly spraying program and stick with it. What we are doing here is putting stuff on your rose leaves that creates an environment that fungal spores can't germinate in. Spores like a rose leaf with a neutral pH. So when we change the pH of the leaf's surface, the spores can't "take root" on it so they can't infect the leaf.

There are a number of helpful fungicides on the market. I used a non-organic, systemic granular fungicide on my roses to help me keep up with the diseases. You simply scrape back the mulch, sprinkle a certain amount around every plant (always read and follow label instructions), and water it in.

One thing: Lime sulfur had been my go-to fungicide for years. Unfortunately, the EPA banned lime sulfur in 2008, so if you've been wondering why you can't find it at your local nursery, that's why. Regular sulfur is still okay, apparently, or copper, or Maneb, but these aren't as handy as lime sulfur. Grumble grumble.

50 Gallons
Lime Sulphur
Solution

Eighty-two rosarians immediately get into a death match over this 50-gallon barrel of lime sulfur.

Here are two homemade remedies for fungal diseases:

Skim milk on your roses is effective against fungal diseases. Yes, skim milk. Mix nine parts water to one part of skim milk (so, 9:1), and spray it on your roses every week. Start spraying as the leaves begin to open, and keep spraying until late fall.

Sodium bicarbonate (baking soda) increases the pH on the leaf's surface, making it more alkaline. Mix one tablespoon of baking soda per gallon of water. Add in a tablespoon of oil, whether it's horticultural oil or vegetable oil, plus a few drops of Ivory dish soap. (The soap lessons the surface tension in each drop of water, allowing the fungicide to spread out on the surface of the leaf instead of beading into droplets.)

Then again, the EPA put the kibosh on Arsenate of Lead because it's a deadly poison ... so there is that.

Spot-Spraying Insects is Best

I don't even spray insects. I just don't! I gave up spraying insecticide after a tragic (it wasn't tragic for me) experience.

When I first started at the rose garden, the previous horticulturist advised me to spray the roses with insecticide every week. So I made up a full sprayer of insecticide and got to work. As soon as I started spraying a ladybug popped out from behind a rose leaf and died. "Sorry!" I said, too late.

Then a praying mantis fell out of a rosebush with a death throttle, dropping the insect she was eating. "Oh no!" I said.

A flock of lacewings, also good guys in the fight against bad insects, shimmered up and perished in the spray, and a honeybee tumbled out of a rose blossom.

"I'm killing all the good bugs!" I wailed. I then returned the sprayer to the tool shed and swore off spraying insecticide. Oh well, that was one less task on my never-ending list o' things to do. Let the good insects do all the work. Fine with me!

So I stopped buying bulk insecticide. Instead I bought a spray bottle of pyrethrum, or one of insecticidal soap (I'd generally grab one or the other when I stopped by the local nursery). When I saw aphids on my roses, I'd spot-spray the bugs that needed spraying. Generally an application or two would do the trick. I also would rub them off with my fingers 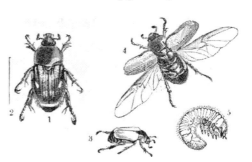 if I didn't have a bottle handy. This approach saved money, it saved time, and it saved the beneficial insects.

Now in the case of Japanese beetles (picture above), it's worth making a gallon of BioNeem spray and knocking those damn bugs out of the ranks of the living. I hate the way that they will mob a rose blossom.

If you have chickens, Japanese beetles are a great feed supplement. My hens love them. Hang a pheromone Japanese beetle trap in the chicken pen, then, every day, empty the bag of beetles into a shallow pan of water to keep the beetles from flying off, and let the chickens eat them up. My hens come running when I bring them Japanese beetles, and after a couple of quick snaps with their beaks, the beetles are history. If you have more beetles than the chickens can eat, freeze them – they'll keep!

The next time someone talks about the "good old days," remember, those were the days that we sprayed our apple trees with arsenic.

Tips For When You Spray

Now, if you do spray chemical insecticides and herbicides, take a few precautions to keep yourself safe.

First, wear proper clothing to keep the spray from coming in contact with your skin. Keith Hawxby, former University Extension specialist for the Northwest region of Missouri, says that standard issue for this includes waterproof shoes, clothing that won't absorb the chemical, and a hat. Neoprene gloves are recommended, since rubber gloves will absorb some chemicals.

Second, **always read and follow label directions**. Chemicals are most effective when they are used in the amounts recommended by the label -- otherwise, it's just extra toxicity for your yard (and for the beneficial critters that live in your soil and grass).

Don't combine chemicals. When mixed, some chemicals simply don't work. Some chemicals when mixed give off poisonous fumes, such as ammonia and bleach. Now, it is true that some chemicals actually work better when combined. HOWEVER: Don't mix chemicals at all unless you have read from a reliable source (label directions, University Extension articles, etc.) that such a mixture is okay.

Third, check wind velocity and direction before you spray to avoid sharing chemical mist with your neighbors or with children. Mr. Hawxby says that the wind speed is difficult to gauge, so it's important to save spraying for calm days. "We want to keep the material on the crop intended, rather than all over the neighborhood," he says. Keep the nozzle of your spray wand close to what you're spraying, generally within a foot of the plant to reduce drift.

Spray only what needs spraying. Otherwise, let the beneficial insects do their work by letting them live.

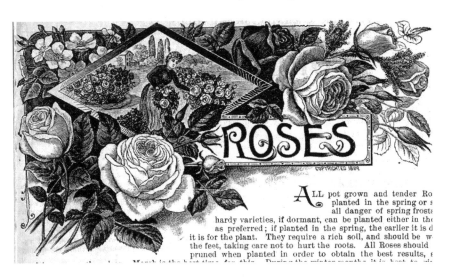

COPYRIGHTED 1889

ALL pot grown and tender Ro
planted in the spring or s
all danger of spring frost:
hardy varieties, if dormant, can be planted either in th(
as preferred; if planted in the spring, the earlier it is d
it is for the plant. They require a rich soil, and should be w
the feet, taking care not to hurt the roots. All Roses should
pruned when planted in order to obtain the best results, :

My roses totally look like this.

Vinegar Makes a Good Herbicide

I get so tired of weeding that I would use dynamite on all the flower beds, except that would be counterproductive.

A good, organically sound solution is to use vinegar to kill weeds. It's non-toxic, a boon to organic growers. The vinegar is biodegradable, so you can spray your weeds, then put down vegetable or grass seeds after they die – there's no harm done to the newly germinating seeds. The acid doesn't linger in the soil, but quickly breaks down.

There are some vinegar herbicides for sale online and at garden centers. Bradfield, and other manufacturers, offers a 20% horticultural vinegar solution that isn't specifically labeled for use on weeds.

In their research report the USDA stated: "WARNING: Note that vinegar with acetic acid concentrations greater than 5% may be hazardous and should be handled with appropriate precautions." So let me put this in stronger terms so there's no mistaking my meaning.

WARNING: If you choose to use 20% vinegar, please be a "safety-first" kind of person and wear goggles, gloves, long sleeves, and shoes when handling or spraying it. Keep away from children and pets. Keep away from eyes and face. If you get any of this stuff on your skin, wash it off quickly. I guarantee you will feel it and it will hurt! When you are finished using it, clean out your spray equipment so it won't get corroded.

And oh yes, always read and follow label instructions *before* using.

Vinegar works best on young growth and annual weeds,

because it burns leaves and tender new growth. It's most effective when you spray the weeds until they are wet, because the vinegar kills only what it touches.

Round-Up (glyphosate) is a *systemic* herbicide; that is, if you spray it on one part of the plant, it will spread through the rest of the plant's system. Vinegar is a *contact* herbicide; it kills only what it touches. That means your application methods will differ between these two herbicides. With Round-Up, I can spray a couple of leaves on a plant, and the herbicide would travel through the whole plant and get the work done. But, since there's some concern that Round-Up could linger in the soil, I would spot-spray each plant, a little squirt for each weed. That generally did the trick.

When spraying vinegar, I'd drench the weed with spray. Be careful of wind blowback because the fumes are powerful. For perennial weeds and grasses, I also put the applicator tip right down on the soil line where the plant met the root and sprayed enough vinegar to let it soak into the soil. This kills off part of the roots and discourages the weed from regenerating.

If you have a large patch of weeds, spray them all at once. After the foliage dies back, clear away the dead stuff. Then spot-spray anything that comes back.

Both herbicides are non-selective; that is, they will kill or cause dieback on whatever plant they touch – whether it's a weed or not! So when spraying, do your best to keep them off your roses and perennials and garden plants.

Horticultural vinegar should be treated with care. This ain't the stuff you put on your salad.

A GALLERY OF BENEFICIAL INSECTS

Lacewings (*Chrysoperla carnea*)

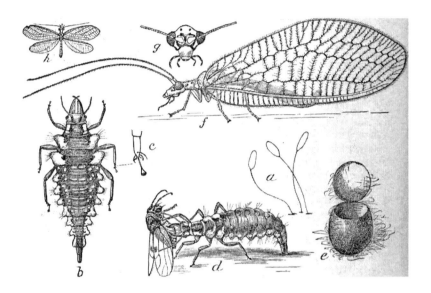

Lacewings (illustration f) look like a skinny green lady in a gigantic shimmering dress. Illustration h gives you an overhead view of a lacewing and its two pairs of wide wings. Lacewings are wonderful predatory insects to have in the garden. Their tiny white eggs (illustration a) are a little bigger than a comma, and are attached to the top of the leaf by a long stem that holds them aloft.

The lacewing nymph that hatches out of the egg (illustrations b and d) are usually a yellowish or red color – and they are voracious predators. They'll even bite humans! I'm ashamed to admit that I used to squash them because those little jerks bit me – but I'm changing my tune now that I know what they are. But they'd better not bite me

Ladybugs (Coccinellidae)

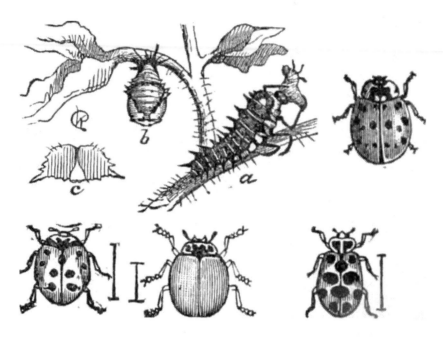

I'm giving the family name of this particular beetle, instead of listing an individual ladybug species, because there are so many ladybeetle species throughout the world, even in Missouri. The ladybug, a beneficial insect, is often red or brown, and often spotted (but not always).

The ladybugs' eggs (not shown) are often tiny and orange. The ladybug larvae (illustration a), which is black with orange markings, is a predator, voraciously attacking aphids like a tiny black and orange dragon. Illustration b shows the larvae pupating to turn into an adult ladybeetle. The adult ladybugs are just as predatory. All of these are great assets in the garden.

Wheel Bugs (*Arilus cristatus*)

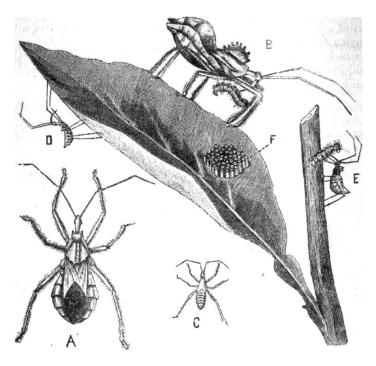

Figure A, adult insect; B, adult insect devouring a caterpillar; C, larva; D. larva; E, larva devouring a caterpillar; F, egg cluster. All enlarged, thank heavens, because the last thing you want to see is a wheelbug the size of your hand coming at you. Wheelbugs are in the Reduviidae family, or the Assassin Bug family. These guys ambush their prey, jab them with their proboscis, and then carry the poor bug around like it's a Slurpee from the 7-11. Don't pick a wheelbug up because they will stab you with that proboscis. They're great to have in the garden, but holy crap don't try to make friends with them. They called "assassin bugs" for a reason!

Praying Mantis (*Mantis religiosa*)

Now these guys are great, and they don't even kill you. Praying mantises are often green or brown and busily eat other insects (and sometimes each other). Also they're fun to play with. If they're sitting on your hand, they'll start swaying back and forth hypnotically, and if you let them do this long enough they will probably jump on your head. Their egg cases, actually a form of solidified foam, look like a brown packing peanut stuck to a twig. When young mantids hatch, they sometimes end up devouring each other, so eager they are to get something to eat. Mantids are sold through garden supply companies to be released in your garden, if you want to build a mantis paradise in your backyard! Or not.

If you put a mantid on your computer screen and start moving the cursor around on the screen, sometimes the mantid will chase it and try to catch it.

A ROGUE'S GALLERY O' BAD ARTHROPODS

Spotted Cucumber Beetles

The spotted cucumber beetle which look like green ladybugs not only can spread diseases to your cucumbers, melons, and cucurbits, but they will also spoil your rose blossoms. Unlike real ladybugs, these spotted green beetles eat the stamens of your rose, then all the petals fall off. They seem to be attracted to the white and yellow roses most of all. Any time I see a beetle, I just grab it in  my fingers and squish it. If you don't want bug guts on your fingers, carry a spray bottle of insecticidal soap and squirt the beetles when you see them.

Spider Mites

Hot and dry weather can lead to a spider mite infestation. Spider mites infect some roses (I had an antique rose called 'Rose de Rescht' that kept catching them), as well as on burning bushes and marigolds. Rose bushes infested with spider mites generally turn a brownish-red, the leaves looking as if the sun burned 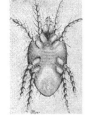 them, or the leaves might look yellowish with green veins. When you turn the leaf over, you may see little webs and some tiny salt-and-pepper grit.

Marigolds infested with spider mites tend to turn whitish in the leaves. In advanced cases, the plant becomes swathed in webs until it turns into a marigold mummy.

Control spider mites with a strong spray from a garden hose from underneath. This disrupts their activity and washes off the dust that hides the mites from natural predators. This will knock some leaves off – but these leaves were going to fall off anyway.

Another way is to spray horticultural oil, or dormant oil, on the affected plant. This suffocates the mites with a thin layer of oil that still allows the plants to breathe. It's also a safe way to kill the mites, as opposed to chemicals. If you spray horticultural or dormant oil, do it when it's cool, to try and keep the leaves from burning. Otherwise, blasting the rose bush often with a powerful spray of water is the best way to go.

Aphids

Aphids, sometimes called plant lice, are tiny sap-sucking insects that appear on soft stems and new foliage. Generally they are green but sometimes you'll see black or wooly white aphids. They reproduce by laying eggs AND through giving live birth AND they don't need to sexually reproduce because females can create baby aphids on their own! Great news, right? or not.

These soft-bodied, tiny insects don't need a protective shell because aphids are protected by ants. When their backs are stroked, aphids secrete honeydew – that is, they put out a little drop of sugar. Ants have figured this out, so when the ants discover that aphids have taken over a plant, the ants will organize and protect the aphids. The ants stroke the aphids' backs to get honeydew, then take the honeydew back to the anthill. Ants "farm" aphids the way a farmer raises dairy cattle. 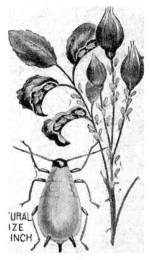 Some species of ants will even carry aphid eggs back to the anthill in fall so the eggs have a safe, warm place to hatch, then put the newly-hatched aphids back onto the plants in spring.

What's more, the honeydew the aphids secrete makes the plant's leaves and stems sticky. The sugary honeydew then causes the plant to catch black sooty mold.

I've stopped an aphid infestation simply by upending a bucket of soapy water over my roses. I did that three times over about a week and that fixed matters pretty well. You can also blast the aphids with a garden hose to clear them out.

I've also followed the ants that were farming the aphids back to their nest, then poured soapy water over the nest as well. That stops the ants. Then beneficial insects like ladybugs, damselflies, praying mantises, and others can move in and eat the aphids up.

For small infestations, spray the aphids with insecticidal soap every three days. Blast them with the water hose every time you water, and rub the aphids off with your fingers.

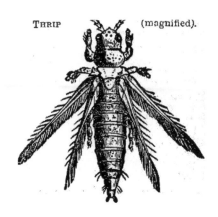

Thrip   (magnified).

Thrips

These tiny insects, which are small enough to be drifted by wind from plant to plant, use a tiny proboscis (i.e. a bug straw) to puncture the leaf and suck out the contents of the cells, causing the surface of the leaf to turn silvery or whitish. When thrips feed on rose petals, you see unsightly brown spots. Unfortunately, by the time you notice these spots, the thrips are usually long gone. They do their damage while the rose blossom is still in bud, so you don't see their work until the flower opens. By then, they've already laid their eggs and died. However, thrips can have as many as eight generations per year, depending on conditions.

Here's an interesting bit of news via *Fine Gardening* magazine. One interesting way to control thrips is to allow aphids to show up on your roses.

According to an organic rose nursery, Bierkreek, the hoverfly (a small fly that disguises itself as a bee, and is often mistaken for a sweat bee) is very beneficial to roses. In spring, the hoverfly lays its eggs near aphids. When the hoverfly larvae hatch out, they eat the aphids. Once these metamorphose into adults, they'll lay their eggs – which hatch when thrips are out and about. And the second generation of hoverfly larvae eat thrips!

So that's yet another reason than ever to not spray indiscriminately for insects.

Encouraging predatory insects are the best way to control thrips in the first place. On hot days, spray your roses with water to wash off the dust that shelters thrips. If you've had trouble with thrips already, you might spray a little bit of Neem oil onto your buds before they open – keep it off already opened flowers, so you don't get any on any visiting honeybees. Spray the buds every other day due to the thrips' fast life cycle.

Cut off and dispose of any thrips-damaged blossoms to get rid of any eggs or thrips that might be on them.

Japanese Beetles

When I was taking care of the rose garden in Missouri, I didn't have any trouble with Japanese beetles. Then I started going to St. Paul, Minnesota every summer, and I was agog at the mobs of Japanese beetles on their rose blossoms. I'd grab the beetles off the rugosas and crush them in my fingers, but just as soon as I turned around there'd be more and more landing on the roses. Ugh! They were like tiny nanobot creatures intent on the destruction of all the world's roses! And worse, they were busy skeletonizing the leaves of various other plants.

FIGURE 2.—The Japanese beetle. X 3

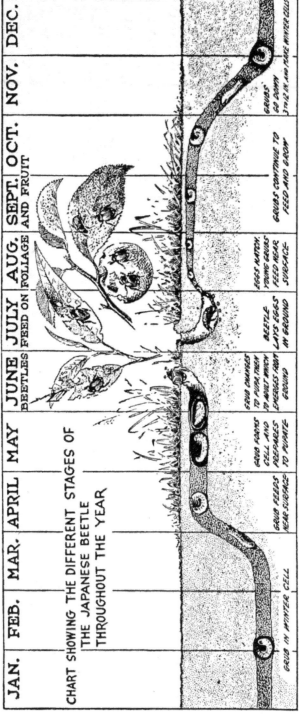

CHART SHOWING THE DIFFERENT STAGES OF THE JAPANESE BEETLE THROUGHOUT THE YEAR

(Japanese beetles, continued)

And now, this year after we had a cold, wet spring, they started showing up in huge numbers on my backyard Missouri roses in June, finally dwindling away in early August. I've seen them in recent years and now they seem to be here to stay.

So what do you do when the nanobot apocalypse looms for your roses?

One way to stop Japanese beetles is to handpicking them. In the early morning, when beetles are sluggish, knock them off your plants into a bucket of soapy water. You can also spray them with Neem oil products. (Be sure these contain azadirachtin, also called BioNeem; also, look for the active ingredient "clarified hydrophobic extracts of neem.") Insecticidal soap is generally ineffective.

It's important to keep handpicking, because when adult Japanese beetles congregate on plants, they attract more and more beetles.

If you have only a few roses, you might wrap your blossoms in cheesecloth to keep the little jerks away from them.

Pheromone traps are a possibility – except that they end up bringing in more Japanese beetles than they kill. These work best if you're able to put them in a place far away from your plants. Empty out the bag daily, because dead beetles really stink.

Again, chickens love to eat Japanese beetles, and you can find various ideas online about how to rig a pheromone trap to feed your hungry flock. Some people make a chute from the pheromone trap to a pan of water. The clumsy beetles fall into the water and struggle until a chicken very happily puts them out of their misery. Apparently some chickens will even jump and catch beetles that are on their way to the pheromone traps.

A nice way to kill two birds (beetles?) with one stone is to wear Spikes of Death (also called Aerator Sandals) around the yard. These aerate your lawn while also killing the Japanese beetle grubs that live in your yard. Use these in April and May – if your lawn has grub problems, you might be able to put a small dent in the local Japanese beetle population, kill off many of the grubs and pupating beetles in your lawn, and aerate your soil.

Leaf-Cutter Bees

Leaf-cutter bees will make an appearance in summer, cutting neat circles in your rose leaves. There's not much you can do about them, as they've generally moved on once you see their damage. Since they're pollinators, and the honeybees need all the pollinating help they can get, spare the leaf-cutter bees. Protect those pollinators, and let the damage go.

A leafcutter bee at work doing her thing.

Fight! Fight! Fight! Fight!

Birds Are On Your Side

One day I was surprised to see a lot of sparrows in the rose garden, hopping around the canes inside the roses. This is odd behavior for house sparrows – usually sparrows will congregate in a large bush that provides cover, or they'll hop around in the open. So I stopped to watch a female sparrow hopping from cane to cane inside a rose bush. With a dart of her head, the female sparrow grabbed something off a leaf and flung it to the ground, then hopped down after it. It was a small green caterpillar, which she quickly ate up. Other sparrows were doing this too.

So the sparrows had noticed that my roses had a caterpillar outbreak and were cleaning them up! I was amazed and pretty grateful. Thanks to the sparrows, there were no signs of caterpillars after that. I was glad I hadn't sprayed for insects.

Somebody should have told me how addicting bird watching is. I bought a copy of *Birds of Missouri*, which is available from the Missouri Department of Conservation, because I was outside a lot and simply wanted to know more about birds.

One afternoon I was shutting off the water in the rose garden when a tiny slate-blue bird perched on the 'Las Vegas' rose about eight feet away. It sat there for about a minute, observing me. I wrote down its description and found out later that it was a Northern Parula, which is a kind of warbler. I'd never heard of it.

Now I'm scanning the skies and listening to my bird calls tape in hopes that I can identify more species. I have check marks in the *Birds of Missouri* book to keep tracks of which birds I have positively identified. I'm going with the flow. I learn a lot when I let myself get excited about a new subject and follow through. Birds are fun.

WHITE BARONESS (H.P.)

'White Baroness,' a sport of 'Baron Rothschild.' (A sport is a mutation of a plant that bears flowers or leaves of a different color or style.) It might possibly be 'Merveille de Lyon,' aka 'Mabel Morrison,' also a white sport of 'Baron Rothschild' introduced in 1882 or 1887.

A rose with rose rosette virus. Note the marked difference between normal canes and the new, hyper-thorny growth. Also compare the old leaves with the new leaves, the old growth with the new. A huge difference between all of these is one of the hallmarks of this virus.

Rose Rosette Disease: No Cure

In December of my first year as horticulturist, I had to get a work crew to help me remove 50 rose bushes, rootballs and all, leaving 50 big craters in the ground. At least there wasn't a whole lot of foot traffic through the garden at that time of year. But my boss collared me after the rose-digging operation started. "What are you doing with those roses?" he asked.

It's a long story.

A great number of the Krug Park roses had a (then) obscure disease called rose rosette virus, which is spread by airborne mites. For this disease, there is no cure; an infected rose will infect other roses, so it must be dug up and thrown away, or burned.

A rose infected by the rose rosette disease (RRD) develops fast-growing canes that look a *lot* different than normal new growth, usually purple- or bronze-red. On some roses, the growth is a sickly lime-green color. In some cases, the thin, needle-like leaves look as if they've been afflicted by powdery mildew. This sudden, odd growth is thicker than the stem it sprouted from, and looks much different from normal new growth. As the disease progresses, new canes are covered with thorns, with many stems emerging from the same place on the cane – a witch's broom. These shoots and their thorns are pliable, almost rubbery. You can bend the shoots almost in half and they won't snap. These shoots are hyperthorny, covered with pliable thorns.

Leaves on infected roses have bumpy or pebbly surfaces; sometimes, they seem to be more leaf-veins than leaf, as if they've suffered severe herbicide damage. Blossoms on infected plants are cabbage-shaped and tiny. Often, they can't open. The color and shape of infected growth seldom resembles healthy parts of the same rose. As the disease progresses, the rose's canes turn black and burned-looking. The rose dies in about two years.

The disease is spread by a type of eriophyid mite (specifically, *Phyllocoptes fructiphilus*), a nearly microscopic carrot-shaped mite that drifts on the wind from one rose to another, and feeds on the surface of leaves. These mites are vectors for the virus – that is, they give the virus a means to travel from plant to plant and infect them. In this case, the mites pick up the virus from an infected plant, then travel to another plant where they start feeding, and spread the virus into the new plant's system. Eriophyid mites are smaller than spider mites, and they do not respond to the same chemical controls.

Multiflora roses – the wild roses that grow along highways all through the country – are highly susceptible to rose rosette disease. Therefore, any roses downwind from a stand of multifloras can pick up eriophyid mites that drift in, even from miles away.

I've had great success with removing infected shoots from my roses as soon as I see them. Often, you can take this new shoot off right where it meets the stem. If the new shoot is pretty big, like it's been growing for a while, then I cut off the cane about six inches down from where it's sprouting out, just in case the virus gotten into the rose. I put the diseased part into a plastic bag, tie it shut, and get it out of the garden. Then I watch any growth from that rosebush to be sure the new growth comes out normal. If you remove the infected part early enough, you can stop the disease in its tracks. Fast action yields great results.

Keep monitoring that particular rose. If new diseased growth starts growing out of that particular cane again, cut it clear off at the bud union. If diseased growth comes out of any other part of the plant, cut that off. Keep doing this until 1) no more diseased growth appears, or 2) until it's obvious that the disease has fully infected the rose, and you have to dig up and destroy the rose. There is no cure.

"Isn't there something you could spray to kill the disease?" one might ask. Unfortunately, there is not. Unlike bacteria, which can be killed by various methods, viruses cannot, because they are, technically, not alive. That's why you can't do much against virus-spread diseases. The only thing you can do is to stop the disease, when possible, and to dig up the infected plants and get them out of the garden.

When you dig up a diseased rose, go deep into the ground. In the past, I dug out all of the old soil around the rose and got rid of that, along with the rose and its roots. Now I think that might have taken things too far. (On the other hand, the rose bushes had been there for a long time, and in that case, you have to get rid of the old soil to reinvigorate it, or the new rose won't grow very well. However, do get rid of as many roots as possible when you dig up the infected rose. An infected root left in the ground could infect a new rose planted in the same place. Also, clear out the top of the soil and any plant litter around the rose to get rid of any mites that might have fallen to the ground and are waiting to infect your new rose.

For more information on the disease, fellow rosarian Ann Peck has an e-book on the Web with plenty of photos at http://www.rosegeek.com/ (I get a little tiny mention in Chapter 15, "Rose Rosette and Public Gardens," as the hapless rose grower south of the Iowa/Missouri state line.)

"Now Nip Rose, Hold up your head and let's see who
is the best girl."

The Wonderful New Rose,— CRIMSON RAMBLER.

COPYRIGHTED 1895

The demand predicted last year for CRIMSON RAMBLER was ww.AB.a.ca. greatly exceeded. Our stock, although the largest in the country, was exhausted by May 1st. For 1896 we have grown double as many plants, and hope to fill all orders with strong plants of last summer's propagation.

Another year's trial adds greatly to our valuation of this splendid Rose, and the enthusiastic praise which pours in from amateurs on all sides proves that it succeeds equally well throughout the country. In hardiness it exceeded our expectations, standing the winter unprotected so well that six-foot canes of last season's growth did not need to be pruned back an inch this spring.

The size and beauty of the flower-heads are truly wonderful. The story of its having three hundred buds to a shoot seemed almost incredible, but last spring *we counted on one shoot four hundred and thirty buds and flowers!*

The rapidity with which the plants grow is also a source of constant wonder. Shoots from eight to ten feet high spring up in one season, while the foliage is so thick and luxuriant that a bower of shade is soon formed. This distinct, handsome foliage remains bright long after other Roses have dropped their leaves. The glorious trusses of glowing crimson flowers appear in June, and remain perfect and undimmed in color for several weeks.

We recommend CRIMSON RAMBLER for five different purposes: As a superb climber for veranda or trellis; for pruning back to handsome specimen clumps; for pegging down in beds; for training over stumps, rocks, and unsightly objects, and for quick-growing screens, hedges, etc.

CRIMSON RAMBLERS.—Our price for this year is 15 cts. each; 4 for 50 cts.; 9

When a Rose Doesn't Bloom

If your rose isn't blooming, there may be several reasons. Perhaps the rose is a newly-planted one – give it some time to get established. Perhaps it's planted in a too-shady location – roses need at least 6 hours of full sun each day. Or maybe it has sprouted shoots from the roots and the original rose you bought has died back. (Many hybrid teas are grafted onto roots from a different rose, a rose which is often better at surviving cold winters than the rose you bought.) Finally, give it a dose of fertilizer that's high in phosphorus to encourage blooms.

A Rose Branch showing the position of the " eyes."

PROPAGATION

Rooting Old Roses

I took cuttings from a rose that is allegedly my Great-great-grandma Chilcote's; I hope they will root. Of course, I'm a sucker for any old rose, and this one seems to be a sweetheart. It has a pink blossom with white in its center and a delicate apple scent. It's also plagued by powdery mildew – but what the heck, nothing is perfect.

It's exciting to own an heirloom, something that one of

your ancestors treated with love. Now you get to care for what they cared for long ago. And I like the thought of saying to my daughter, "This is a rose your great-great-great-great grandma grew, allegedly." It's mind-boggling, but really neat.

I'm also trying to get cuttings off an old rose that used to grow by the Nodaway Depot. It's a once-a-year bloomer, but it has these tiny purple blossoms that smell really sweet, as violet as I've ever seen a rose. It's a big old shrub, but those flowers are lovely. (NOTE: The cuttings didn't take, and I didn't go back and take more – and then the rose died after the drought of 2011. Don't be like me. Take action to save the past. Nothing lasts forever.)

SOUVENIR DE WOOTTON

The 'Souvenir de Wootton' (1888), as far as we know, has one plant of this particular variety still alive. Rosarians are taking cuttings of it to bring it back. Long may it grow!

How to take cuttings

The best times to take softwood rose cuttings is in spring and in fall, when the plant cells are most active. Choose pliable soft-wooded shoots with at least four leaf buds on them – about four or five inches long – and strip off all but the top leaf. Some rosarians state that the cuttings are more likely to take if they have a "heel" – that is, a bit of the woody stem that the shoot came off of – attached at its base.

Morning is the best time to take cuttings, if possible. The

rose stems are full of water then. Always take more rose cuttings than you need. Propagation is an imperfect art, relying on the vagaries of weather, watering, disease, and the temperament of the rose itself.

 Something that might help the rose cuttings take root is willow water. This is how to make it. Fill a bucket with a few inches of water, then cut a couple of willow shoots into matchstick-sized pieces and drop them in the bucket. Let them soak overnight. The next day, when you take the rose cuttings, soak the bottom three inches of these cuttings in this water for several hours. The willow contains a rooting hormone that encourages the rose cuttings to start developing roots. (This rooting hormone, by the way, is the reason why you can cut a willow wand, stick it into the ground, and it will root almost right away.)

Of course, instead of willow water you could use rooting powder. Dip the cutting in rooting solution and pot it in a 4 or 6 inch pot in a mix of sand and peat moss. Plant it with two buds under the ground and at least two above. (See picture below.) Wrap the pot and cutting in a clear plastic bag and tie it shut. Keep it in a shaded location so the sun doesn't burn the heck out of the bagged rose. Check the soil and make sure it stays moist.

Rooting roses takes mainly shade, coolness, and moist rooting medium. I have successfully rooted roses in moist peat moss in a wheelbarrow left in a cool tool shed. (I'd put them there and had forgotten about them until I needed the extra wheelbarrow.)

Roots form in two to four weeks. Remove the bag when

roots are two inches long. After that, fertilize the cuttings with a weak kelp emulsion fertilizer, half strength, about once a month. (Other liquid fertilizers work, too, just as long as they're at half-strength.) Check for roots near the surface now and then. When you start seeing them, transplant it into a bigger pot with regular soil mix and move it outside. Early fall is a good time to plant the rose in your garden. Mulch it well when winter comes.

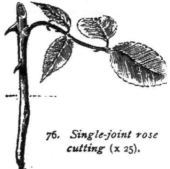

76. *Single-joint rose cutting* (x 25).

You don't even have to do all of the above to take a cutting. In *The Amateur's Practical Garden-Book* (1900), the author states: *"The writer has known women who could root Roses with the greatest ease. They would simply break off a branch of the Rose, insert it in the flower-bed, cover it with a bell-jar, and in a few weeks they would have a strong plant."* So perhaps all you have to do is cut off a stem, stick it in the ground, and put a Mason jar over it, and get roots after a couple of weeks. How appealingly simple!

A layered plant. Note that the stem under the ground has been cracked, and is being held down by a peg. In this case, the upright stem is staked to get it to grow straight into the air instead of leaning crookedly any which way.

Layering Roses

Another way to propagate a rose is through layering. In this method, the plant is still attached to the parent, so it's easier to keep watered and alive while the roots are growing.

The best time to layer plants is in February and March, before plant growth starts, and then again in June and July, once the sap is going in the plants.

Take a pliable cane and bend it to the ground. Make a small cut on the cane where it touches the soil, just below a bud eye. Bury the cut portion in about four inches of dirt, and put a brick on it so it won't pop out of the ground. Or you can use a forked stick to "peg down" the layer. Water the soil every week. After three or four weeks, the shoot should have rooted, and you should see the branch start to grow. That's how you know that your layer has formed roots.

You will have to wait a year for your new rose plant to get to a decent size, so be patient. When the rose has enough roots, plant it in a sunny location, digging plenty of rotted manure and compost into the ground around it.

Where To Find Old Roses

If you're really crazy for old roses – their fragrance, their romance – visit old cemeteries, abandoned homesteads, and old farms to see if you can find more. Many of these old roses, now nameless, once had an amazing past before they got pushed out of commerce by modern roses and hybrid teas and forgotten. Rose wranglers, or rose rustlers, collect old roses like these and have brought them back into gardens for all to admire. The Antique Rose Emporium in Tyler, Texas, sells many roses that have been rescued by these wranglers (and they look amazing).

But remember to always, always get permission if the rose is on private property. Be courteous to the rose owner. Offer to share clippings with them if they would like. Make a good name for yourself and for other rose wranglers.

MONTH-BY-MONTH CHECKLISTS

Note: These dates are best for Zones 5 and 6. If you live in a different USDA zone (the map is in the back of this book), or overseas, consult a local rosarian or your local University Extension center. They'll get you up to speed right away.

JANUARY

* Make a resolution to keep a garden notebook. (Read my article about gardening notebooks in *Don't Throw in the Trowel! Vegetable Gardening Month by Month.*) A gardening notebook, used in

conjunction with a calendar, can be the biggest help you have in a garden.

* Don't add wood ashes to your rose garden without first knowing the pH of the soil. Ashes will, over time, raise the pH of your soil. Roses do like soil to be a little on the acidic side, though they do fine with soils that range from 6.0 to 7.0 pH (a normal soil tests at 7.0). If your soil test comes back with a higher pH (i.e. a more alkaline, or sweeter, soil), then you might add ashes to your garden now and then, and retest the soil next fall to see how much the pH has changed.

Protip: When it comes to pH, the lower the number is, the more acidic the soil.

* Check your tools to be sure everything is sharpened and oiled. You might be surprised by rust on some tools if they were improperly put away last fall. It's better to be surprised now than in early spring. Rub the wooden handles of your tools with paraffin. Check the tire on your wheelbarrow to see if it needs aired or replaced. You might even give the wheelbarrow a fresh coat of paint if it's starting to get rust spots.

*Once the weather warms up, spray horticultural oil on your fruit trees, raspberry canes, and roses (if the roses aren't completely covered up).

What is horticultural oil? This is a light oil that kills insects by suffocating them. Horticultural oil also penetrates the shells of insect eggs and wrecks their metabolic and respiratory processes. It used to be that you couldn't spray horticultural oils on plants outside of winter because it would burn leaves. These days, most horticultural oils are refined enough to where they shouldn't injure most plants during their growing season.

Horticultural oils – and dormant oils, which are sprayed during winter, the dormant season for plants – are different than Neem oils, which come from the seeds of the Neem tree. Neem oils have a wider range of use, being effective at killing insects and their eggs, certain mite eggs, while helping prevent blackspot and powdery mildew.

The roses will also benefit from a dose of copper once a month. Studies have shown that roses sprayed with copper through the winter have less disease through the year.

Of course, being able to spray when the weather is halfway decent is a challenge. "Hey, boss, I'm going home the rest of the day to spray my roses, bye!" Not in our lifetime.

* Water your outside plants, which lose moisture through their stems and their buds. Of course, do this when the temps are above 32 degrees!

Just ... don't use Arsenate of Lead like this gentleman is doing.

FEBRUARY

* Spray dormant oil on the roses when the temperatures are above freezing. Dormant oil controls scale and other insect pests on roses as well as pines, magnolias, and fruit trees.

* Check roses for frost heaving. If the freezing and thawing temperatures have caused your rose roots to be pushed up out of the ground, gently tamp them back in and add a nice, thick layer of mulch to keep soil temperatures at a more constant level.

* Don't dig in wet soils!

BARONESS ROTHSCHILD (H.P.)

'Baroness Rothschild' (1868), a repeat-blooming shell-pink rose. Has some fragrance. Widely available.

MARCH

* You can plant bare-root roses now, just as long as the ground where you're planting isn't frozen. If you buy them through the mail, unwrap the dormant plants immediately. Put the rose roots into some moistened peat moss or soilless mix, cover them with plastic to keep the canes from drying out, and store them in a cool location. Plant them as soon as possible.

* You might start watering plants, especially if the winter has been dry. This will help them as they gear up for spring.

* It's an especially good time for spring clean-up. Rake the leaves and trim the dead canes off the roses. Start taking mulch off the roses about mid-way through the month.

* Stop applying dormant oil now that the buds are swelling and new shoots are appearing on the roses. Dormant oil can damage these.

* A lot of winter weeds can be pulled now – some of the low-growing weeds already have little blue flowers. You can also use vinegar to kill off some of the annual weeds such as henbit (the purple flowering one) and chickweed (which is edible). The perennial weeds will grow back, so keep hitting them until they die from exhaustion.

You can buy herbicidal vinegar in some garden or retail stores. Keep in mind, however, that the herbicidal vinegar contains 10 to 20 percent acid – it will burn your eyes and skin. Always wear eye and skin protection when using this vinegar.

APRIL

* Get a new pair of rose gauntlets if you need them. These are gloves with a long sleeve that protects your arms. If you're super tough and don't mind your arms looking like they'd been attacked by feral cats, then wear regular gloves while working with roses. (Actually, you can learn how to work with roses while wearing regular gloves if you're a real safety-first kind of gal. I did for years. Sometimes I'd find a thorn in my arm and be all like, "Oh, what's that doing there?"

* Start uncovering roses by removing all mulch, or by watering away soil or compost you've mounded up around the canes. (Use your hands to do this, instead of the hoe.) Keep the mulch nearby, just in case there's frost in the forecast so you can quickly cover it back up again.

* Prune out damaged or dead growth, and clean

up the inside of the rose but removing canes that cross each other.

* When the new growth is two inches long, then top-dress the rose (that is, sprinkle it around the base of the rose) with organic, slow-release fertilizer such as Milorganite or Bradfield. Add in compost as well, and cultivate it into the soil. Compost adds a few nutrients, but also adds organic material to the soil, which roses love.

* Cut back floribundas and tea roses to encourage new growth. Usually, I cut them back to about 12 inches if there is a lot of green on the canes. If there's less green, I cut the canes so they are shorter, but generally when I do this I find out that there was more green than I thought. Obviously you can't reattach a rose cane when you cut too much of it off. The best course of action is to cut the cane back to 12 inches, see how much green is showing on the cane, THEN cut it back farther if the inside of the cane is brown.

* Put up a rain gauge near your garden so you

can see how much rain you get every week. If you get an inch or more of rain during the week, you can skip watering.

* Set up your soaker hoses or drip irrigation systems and start watering once a week (unless the rain gauge tells you otherwise).

* Fertilize the roses around April 15 to 20 (if the weather will let you), and spray the plant, and the ground around it, with fungicide to zap blackspot and other fungal diseases.

MAY

* Start spraying roses, but only with fungicides. I never spray insecticides unless I see an actual outbreak of pests, and then I only spot-treat. All insecticides do is damage the population of beneficial insects.

I prefer using a systemic fungicide on roses. A systemic fungicide is usually sprinkled into the soil around the plant roots, and the chemicals are absorbed into the rose, protecting the leaves from the inside against fungal diseases. Rugosa roses usually react badly to spraying, but I've found that they will take systemic fungicide without any trouble. This fungicide also helps keep the roses clean longer, in case you miss a week or two of spraying due to rain or other events. The very nice thing about systemics is that you don't have to reapply the chemical every time it rains. Once it's down in the soil, it works for several months. Always read and follow label instructions.

* Try not to trim the roses when they're wet. Spores of fungal diseases will cling to your hand and pruners and will travel from plant to plant this way. Wait until leaves are dry to trim.

* Be on the lookout for little white caterpillars with black heads on your roses this month. These are called "rose slugs" (they are not slugs  but actually wasp larvae – confusing, I know). These are the larvae for the sawfly, a type of small wasp. In Missouri, sawfly species includes the European roseslug sawfly (*Endelomyia aethiops*), the bristly roseslug sawfly (*Cladius difformis*), and the curled roseslug sawfly (*Allantus cinctus*).

Some sawfly larvae eat the rose leaves from underneath, leaving only the waxy leaf coating, so it looks like your rose leaves have little white patches on them. Blast your roses from underneath with a hard spray of water to knock the wasp larvae off. Let the rose dry. Then follow up with a little spot-spraying with pyrethrum, insecticidal soap, or Neem oil to kill off any extra larvae.

* Follow all the directions above if you see aphids or other insect infestations.

* Set up a birdbath in your rose garden

(preferably near a large shrub or tree) to attract birds. They can help you with insect problems.

* Start giving roses a 20-20-20 liquid fertilizer when the flower buds form.

* If you see an infestation of insects or spider mites, get the water hose and blast them. Sometimes all you need to do to stop an infestation is to blast them off the plant. Later, if you still see some insects, spot-spray them with a little pyrethrin – squish them, too, before you spray. A few passes should do the trick.

* Epsom salts, which are a good source of magnesium, are great in the garden. Add ½ cup of Epsom salts to the soil around the rosebush once a year. This encourages basal breaks – buds that become strong, new canes.

JUNE

* Keep spraying roses with fungicide every week. Spraying fungicide this time of year is crucial in the fight against blackspot and powdery mildew. Pick off badly infected leaves and destroy them.

A systemic fungicide might help, too, because with a systemic, you could miss a spraying and be all right. (Systemics are absorbed into the plant, while other fungicides sit on the surface of the leaf and get washed off with water.)

* Feed your roses every other week (even if it

doesn't seem like it's doing any good), and keep giving them lots of water every week, unless you get over an inch of water in rain.

* A dose of compost, rotted manure, or worm castings around the roots of your roses will help repel diseases and insects though good nutrition, which includes feeding the creatures that live in the soil around the rose's roots. Feed the soil and you get a stronger plant.

* Deadhead flowers once the blossoms fade or shatters. (A rose "shatters" when all its petals start to fall off.) Look for a the first unfurling shoot underneath the old blossom, and cut the flower off just above the new growth.

* Watch for bagworms feeding on many garden plants, but especially juniper and arborvitae. I see them on roses, now and then, in a bag made of little bits of rose leaves. Just take the bagworms off and squish them. If you squish them in your fingers, hold the bag away from your body, because sometimes green goop will squirt out of one end or the other. Trust me, you don't want to be squirted in the face with

bagworm goop.

* Throw some more mulch on the roses that need it. Hot soil stresses a plant, but when you put a nice layer of mulch on and cool the soil, the rose will perk up in a very gratifying way.

ueen of
ses_____
American

JULY

* Japanese beetles are a real pain in the neck. Read the article on page 78 for tips on how to deal with them. If you have chickens or poultry, feed them the beetles for a special treat.

* Keep the birdbath filled and clean for the birds in your rose garden. They'll appreciate this when it's especially dry – and they'll help with pest control on your roses.

*After your rambling and climbing roses get done blooming, cut them back hard to encourage more bloom and better branching.

* Watch for spider mites on your roses now when it gets hot and dry. (See the article about

spider mites on page 74.)

   * Blackspot and powdery mildew can run rampant this time of year. Clip off badly-infected leaves and remove them from the garden. Keep spraying fungicide.

   * Roses can be affected by drought, and could scorch and also suffer from heat stress. Water roses weekly, even if it rains. On hot days, spray the foliage. This serves the double purpose of getting rid of insect infestations and also cools the leaves in the summer heat.

   * Mulch! Mulch! Mulch!

   * Give roses their last application of fertilizer this month. Your fertilization program should end on August 1 to allow the rose to harden up and get ready for winter. However, putting down compost is still okay. (Some rosarians will keep applying a dilute fertilizer to keep up the flower display, especially those who are running public gardens.)

   * Green ladybugs (spotted cucumber beetles) will be crawling around in your rose from now until the end of the year, eating around the stamens and making your rose petals fall off. Squish the bugs in your fingers.

AUGUST

* Some of your red roses might have turned brown-white on the tops of the blossoms. That's sunburn. The darker the red of the rose, the more heat it soaks up from the sun, which burns the petals. Ruined blossoms should be cut off.

* Some roses might also suffer from leaf scorch or heat stress. Keep them well-watered so they don't succumb to stress.

* Also, due to the heat, roses generally fall into a semi-dormant state during the hottest month of the year, so blooming and growth will slow down. You aren't willing to be active in hot weather; why

should roses be any different?

* Fertilize the roses one last time in August, but only at a half-dose. No nitrogen fertilizer after August 15, or the soft, new growth that nitrogen produces will turn black when the first freeze hits.

* Soak your roses to a depth of ten inches during the hottest part of the summer. (I would generally turn on the soaker hoses for at least a few hours and give the roses a good long drink that way.)

* Keep up on watering and spraying fungicides. Your roses will reward you for your patience when the weather cools in September.

* Watch for spider mite activity, and blast them off the rose with the hose.

* Japanese beetle damage should taper off, because this is the time that adults will lay eggs in the soil and die. Kill off as many beetles as possible to keep them from laying eggs in the ground.

* For goodness' sake, stay cool out there. August heat, coupled with 95 percent relative humidity, can be brutal. Drink plenty of water, wear a wide-brimmed hat to keep the sun off, and take breaks in the shade if you can. If you feel ill, nauseated, dizzy, or lightheaded, go sit down and have a cool drink. Heatstroke and heat exhaustion are very real dangers. Take care of yourself.

Grand Novelty. New Striped Rose.
— Vick's Caprice. —

'Vick's Caprice' (before 1889) is a subtly striped pink-and-white rose. Mostly thornless and mostly upright. Available commercially.

SEPTEMBER

There have been a few days that have been so downright cool that I think that it's already autumn, and that there's maybe hope for us yet. Apple season has started, too. Hooray for fall!

* Now that the heat is letting up, the roses will be coming back with some great sprays of blossoms, as well as more growth.

* Stop deadheading the roses (removing spent blossoms) by Sept. 15. The rose will then set hips,

another signal that they need to get ready for winter.

* This is a good time to replace your roses if you have any gaps in your rose garden, or if you have a rose that's just been a real dog and doesn't want to grow, or if it grows too much and keeps grabbing you with its thorny arms, even when you're halfway across the garden from it. When you dig up a rose, rosarians jokingly call this "shovel pruning."

Though the selection is limited, roses are cheap this time of year. Also, planting now allows roses to get established before next summer dries them out. Be sure to give them a decent mulch this fall so they get through winter all right.

* This is also a good time to clean up all those weeds you couldn't get to this summer. Bring along a pair of pruners for the small trees that have gotten a roothold in your gardens. Sometimes, if the ground's really wet after a good rain, and if you're really tough, you can actually pull the tree seedlings out, root and all. More often, though, you'll have to clip it at ground level. Or dig it out with a shovel so you don't have to keep cutting it year after year.

* Rose rosette disease can show up on your roses at any time during the growing season, but now that new growth is coming in, it can be especially noticeable. Keep an eye out for unusual, fast growth on your roses that doesn't look anything like the other new growth coming out of that rose. Refer to the article on page 84 for more information.

* Roses are contrary; they don't ever listen to a

thing you say. So don't be surprised if they keep on blooming right up through November, despite your having done all the right things. They just want to show off. And they will, too. They don't care what you think.

Known as 'Triomph de Pernet Père,' (1890), a cherry-magenta blossom, strong tea fragrance, floriferous. Still available.

OCTOBER

* There's still plenty of time to plant potted roses in October. Their roots will be in the ground, safe from winter's cold, and the roots will grow over the winter. But when spring hits, these roses will pick right up and start growing, and you won't have to bother with all that spring mud and slush.

* In October, clip the buds off the roses. I hate to take the buds off, especially if the roses have been blooming beautifully. However, they need to prepare for winter, not expend energy in blooms that will be blasted by frost. (But sometimes I just let 'em grow. Despite what the boss rosarians say, I'd rather enjoy my blossoms as long as possible, thanks!)

* When all the rose canes are bare, remove out any excess canes, leaving only healthy, large canes. Then spray the canes and the ground around them with dormant oil on a warm afternoon to keep blackspot and other diseases from overwintering.

* Rake rose leaves from under your rosebushes. Many diseases and insect eggs survive the winter in old leaves. Burn the leaves.

Keep in mind that if your roses had tobacco mosaic, burning or composting the leaves will not kill the virus, because the viruses can survive incredible temperatures. Tobacco mosaic is the reason you shouldn't crush out a cigarette in your garden. If a tobacco plant infected with the virus got into that cigarette, its ashes will pass the virus on to your roses. This applies especially to plants in the nightshade family, such as potatoes and tomatoes. Members of the rose family (apples, hawthorn trees) are also susceptible -- though they seem to be susceptible to everything anyway.

'White La France,' also known as 'Augustine Guinoisseau' (1889) with flowers white to shell-pink and a delightful tea fragrance. Still in commerce.

NOVEMBER

* An application of Wilt-Pruf will keep roses from losing moisture (this also goes for evergreens, azaleas and rhododendrons).

* Spray roses with their autumnal dose of copper or Maneb to keep blackspot and other diseases from overwintering on the canes and leaves, so you will have less disease trouble next year.

* November is the time to winterize your roses and tuck them in for their long winter's nap. Roses that need winter protection include hybrid teas, miniature, floribunda, multifloras, some climbing roses, and newly planted roses. Many shrub roses won't need as much winter protection (though it's helpful to mulch the roots well).

The time to do the job is after you've had several days of 20 degree weather.

Hybrid teas can be pruned back to knee height, and other roses can also be pruned back. Or, if you prefer, trim them only a little, just enough to cut canes back a little. I prefer not cutting roses back, but get rid of skinny canes, broken canes, and canes that cross each other, and let everything else go. However, old-fashioned roses that bloom once a year shouldn't be pruned at this time – they have their blossoms for next spring all ready to go, deep in their buds. If you cut them back now, you'll cut off their spring flowers. The same goes for climbing roses.

Once the roses are all pruned, then march out there with your Styrofoam cones or peat moss, wood chips, or compost and soil. (Refer back to the article on page 55 for more about getting roses ready for winter.) Pile about 12 to 18 inches of the mulch of your choice over the base of the rose. You can also cage the roses with chicken wire and fill the cages with shredded leaves. Styrofoam cones, once they're placed over the rose, should be weighed down by a rock or a brick or some other weight.

* This is the best time to take soil samples. I have a full article on the subject in my Vegetable Gardening book (*Don't Throw in the Trowel! Vegetable Gardening Month by Month*). Contact your local University Extension service, get a little box/bag, and follow their instructions to the letter for best results. After you give them your soil and pay a little fee, you'll get a paper back telling you what minerals are in your soil and how much organic matter your soil has, along with suggestions about how to improve your soil.

Amend your soil over the winter according to the directions in your soil report, adding lime (to lower pH) or sulfur (to raise pH) and compost (to add organic matter to your soil).

I LOVE FLOWERS. DON'T YOU?

'Madame Hoste' (1888) A pale-yellow hybrid tea, deeper in the center, good form, and very free. No longer available.

Appendix

USDA Zone map – Find this at
http://planthardiness.ars.usda.gov/PHZMWeb/

Type the link above for an interactive, full-color map that allows you to see what zone you live in. You can also click on your home state for a closer look at your local zones. The USDA map on the next page is not as clear as I'd like it to be (because everything in this book is printed in black and white) but it's better than nothing. This map was updated in 2012, but the climate keeps changing.

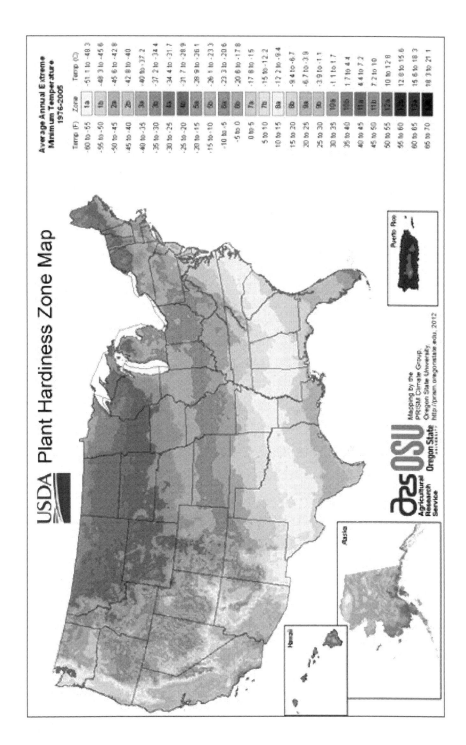

ANTIQUE ROSE SOURCES

The Antique Rose Emporium
https://www.antiqueroseemporium.com/
A great variety of antique roses mixed in with some new varieties, and a number of unknown roses that were rediscovered by rose wranglers, who go out in search of old varieties whose names have been forgotten over time.

Azalea House Flowering Shrub Farm
http://www.floweringshrubfarm.com/
A small operation out of New York state, but they have an amazing selection of antique roses.

Heirloom Roses
http://www.heirloomroses.com/
Roses both old and new.

High Country Roses
https://www.highcountryroses.com/
Many new roses and old roses too.

Rose Petals Nursery
http://www.rosepetalsnursery.com/
A little rose specialty nursery in Florida. Many old varieties.

Rogue Valley Roses
https://www.roguevalleyroses.com/
Some grand old roses here.

Roses of Yesterday and Today
http://www.rosesofyesterday.com/ourroses.html
Many old and antique roses here.

Heritage Rose Foundation
http://www.heritagerosefoundation.org/
A nonprofit organization, established in 1986, dedicated to the preservation of old roses.

FREE PREVIEWS OF MY OTHER GARDENING BOOKS

This sample is the introduction from *Don't Throw in the Trowel: Vegetable Gardening Month by Month*, available through Amazon.

Save Time and Trouble With Garden Journals

When I worked as a municipal horticulturist, I took care of twelve high-maintenance gardens, and a number of smaller ones, over I-don't-know-how-many square miles of city, plus several hundred small trees, an insane number of shrubs, a greenhouse, and whatever else the bosses threw at me. I had to find a way to stay organized besides waking up at 3 a.m. to make extensive lists. My solution: keep a garden journal.

Vegetable gardeners with an organized journal

can take control of production and yields. Whether you have a large garden or a small organic farm, it certainly helps to keep track of everything in order to beat the pests, make the most of your harvest, and keep up with spraying and fertilizing.

Keeping a garden journal reduces stress because your overtaxed brain won't have to carry around all those lists. It saves time by keeping you focused. Writing sharpens the mind, helps it to retain more information, and opens your eyes to the world around you.

My journal is a small five-section notebook, college ruled, and I leave it open to the page I'm working on at the time. The only drawback with a spiral notebook is that after a season or two I have to thumb through a lot of pages to find an earlier comment. A small three-ring binder with five separators would do the trick, too. If you wish, you can take out pages at the end of each season and file them in a master notebook.

I keep two notebooks – one for ornamentals and one for vegetables. However, you might prefer to pile everything into one notebook. Do what feels comfortable to you.

These are the five sections I divide my notebooks into – though you might use different classifications, or put them in different orders. Don't sweat it; this ain't brain surgery. Feel free to experiment. You'll eventually settle into the form that suits you best.

First section: To-do lists.

This is pretty self-explanatory: you write a list, you cross off almost everything on it, you make a new list.

When I worked as horticulturist, I did these lists monthly. I'd visit all the gardens I took care of. After looking at anything left unfinished on the previous month's list, and looking at the garden to see what else needed to be done, I made a new, comprehensive list.

Use one page of the to-do section for reminders of things you need to do next season. If it's summer, and you think of some chores you'll need to do this fall, make a FALL page and write them down. Doing this has saved me lots of headaches.

Second section: Reference lists.

These are lists that you'll refer back to on occasion.

For example, I'd keep a list of all the yews in the parks system that needed trimmed, a list of all gardens that needed weekly waterings, a list of all places that needed sprayed for bagworms, a list of all the roses that needed to be babied, etc.

I would also keep my running lists in this section, too – lists I keep adding to.

For instance, I kept a list of when different vegetables were ready for harvest – even vegetables I didn't grow, as my friends and relatives reported to me. Then when I made a plan for my veggie garden, I would look at the list to get an idea of when these plants finished up, and then I could figure out when I could take them out and put in a new crop. I also had a list of "seed-to-harvest" times, so I could give each crop enough time to make the harvest date before frost.

You can also keep a wish list – plants and vegetables you'd like to have in your garden.

Third section: Tracking progress.

This is a weekly (or, "whenever it occurs to me to write about it") section as well.

If you plant seeds in a greenhouse, keep track of what seeds you order, when you plant them, when they germinate, how many plants you transplant (and how many survive to maturity), and so forth.

When you finish up in the greenhouse, use these pages to look back and record your thoughts – "I will never again try to start vinca from seeds! Never!! Never!!!" Then you don't annoy yourself by forgetting and buying vinca seeds next year.

You can do the same thing when you move on to the vegetable garden – what dates you tilled the ground, planted the seeds, when they germinated, and so forth. Make notes on yields and how everything tasted. "The yellow crooknecks were definitely not what I'd hoped for. Try yellow zucchini next year."

Be sure to write a vegetable garden overview at season's end, too. "Next year, for goodness' sake, get some 8-foot poles for the beans! Also, drive the poles deeper into the ground so they don't fall over during thunderstorms."

During the winter, you can look back on this section and see ways you can improve your yields and harvest ("The dehydrator worked great on the apples!"), and you can see which of your experiments worked.

Fourth section: Details of the natural world.

When keeping a journal, don't limit yourself to what's going on in your garden. Track events in the natural world, too. Write down when the poplars start shedding cotton or when the Queen's Anne Lace blooms.

You've heard old gardening maxims such as "plant corn when oak leaves are the size of a squirrel's ear," or "prune roses when the forsythia blooms." If the spring has been especially cold and everything's behind, you can rely on nature's cues instead of a calendar when planting or preventing disease outbreaks.

Also, by setting down specific events, you can look at the journal later and say, "Oh, I can expect little caterpillars to attack the indigo plant when the Johnson's Blue geranium is blooming." Then next year, when you notice the buds on your geraniums, you can seek out the caterpillar eggs and squish them before they hatch. An ounce of prevention, see?

When I read back over this section of the journal, patterns start to emerge. I noticed that Stargazer lilies bloom just as the major heat begins. This is no mere coincidence: It's happened for the last three years! So now when I see the large buds, I give the air conditioner a quick checkup.

Fifth section: Notes and comments.

This is more like the journal that most people think of as being a journal – here, you just talk about the garden, mull over how things are looking, or grouse about those supposedly blight-resistant tomatoes that decided to be contrary and keel over from blight.

I generally put a date on each entry, then ramble on about any old thing. You can write a description of the garden at sunset, sketch your peppers, or keep track of the habits of bugs you see crawling around in the plants. This ain't art, this is just fun stuff (which, in the end, yields great dividends).

Maybe you've been to a garden talk on the habits of Asian melons and you need a place to put your notes. Put them here!

This is a good place to put garden plans, too. Years later I run into them again, see old mistakes I've made, and remember neat ideas I haven't tried yet.

Get a calendar.

Then, when December comes, get next year's calendar and the gardening journal and sit down at the kitchen table. Using last year's notes, mark on the calendar events to watch out for -- when the tomatoes first ripen, when the summer heat starts to break, and when you expect certain insects to attack. In the upcoming year, you just look at the calendar and say, "Well, the squash bugs will be hatching soon," so you put on your garden gloves and start smashing the little rafts of red eggs on the plants.

A garden journal can be a fount of information, a source of memories, and most of all, a way to keep organized. Who thought a little spiral notebook could do so much?

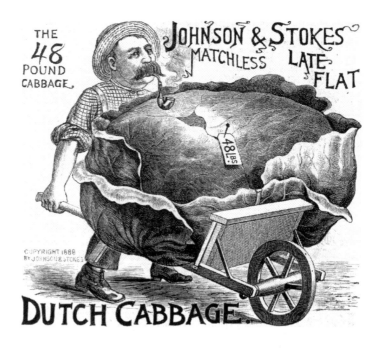

This is the first chapter from *Perennial Classics: Planting and Growing the Best Perennial Garden Ever.*

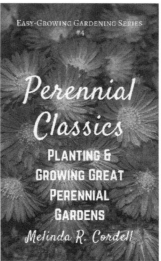

INTRODUCTION
WHY ARE PERENNIALS HARD TO BEAT?

When I was in college, I hit a rough patch and had to drop out. I was working two part-time jobs while taking full-time classes, paying for rent, food, and college (I had no financial aid), while living on ramen and hot dogs. (Fun fact: Due to my poverty diet, the iron levels in my blood were so low that I was not allowed to give blood.) Also, I kept wanting to change majors – I wanted to be an English major, but I kept being told that I needed to get a major that I could earn money in. "You can't make a living out of writing books." So I came back home and started living in my old hometown of Nodaway.

I got a job at a garden center. I had a great boss and co-workers. We would sing while grooming the plants (when I say "grooming the plants," I mean picking the dead leaves and old flowers off the plants – we weren't brushing the plants' hair or anything). We had a lot of good stuff to talk about, and we helped customers find what they wanted, and when they had gardening questions and we didn't know the answers, we'd do everything we could to find the answer. It was a great deal.

The nice thing about working at a garden center is that you get a lot of free plants. Every day you'd work through the flats and pots, and if you saw any plants that were dying or droopy or looked bad, you'd take them out. Some of them just needed a little tender loving care, so those would go to the "plant hospital," as we called it, where they would get a little attention and to perk up. Some of these would recover enough to go back on the tables, but some just sat there looking mopey, so we got to take these home.

I had a bit of a garden where I lived, but now I had a lot of garden. I wasn't very interested in annuals, because they were there for a season and that was it for them. But I loved the perennials. After all these years, I'm trying to put my finger on why they appealed so much to me. I think it was because everybody grew the same annuals over and over – marigolds, geraniums, petunias – but perennials weren't as common. I always go for stuff that's a little uncommon.

Another part of it was that some of these perennials could be true heirlooms in the garden, growing for years and years. I really wanted to grow a Gas Plant (*Dictamnus albus*) because they could stay alive for decades. Alas, the ones we had were just not in very good shape, and I didn't have much luck getting them started in my garden.

At the time, too, I was a little tired of the sameness of all the annuals. Granted, I would change my mind later, when I was working as a city horticulturist, because annuals were such a help in coloring up my flower beds fast. But give me a break, I was in college, and at that time I was just a teeny bit pretentious. Okay, more than a teeny bit.

I also loved the variety of perennials. I had some Connecticut Blue delphiniums that bloomed in the most gorgeous shades of blue I'd ever seen in a plant. I had a Japanese anemone that was a whirligig of white flowers until a bunch of blister beetles ate it up. The jerks. Sea thrift, with its little powderpuff flowers growing out of a tuft of grass; Nepeta, or catmint, with its purple flowers. My cat was nuts about catnip, but she had no interest whatsoever in catmint. I planted some dahlia tubers and got some fascinating, gigantic flowers. A perennial hibiscus startled me with magenta flowers as big as dinner plates. Grandma Mary wanted to know what these plants were! And she is wise in all things plant, so that's saying something.

Now, bringing home a bunch of random plants from the nursery doesn't exactly make for an orderly garden. But I didn't care. I loved most the anticipation – of putting this sad, sickly little plant in the ground and giving it good soil and watering it regularly, and generally the plant would perk up and start growing, and the next year it would start flowering, and whoa! So that's what the flowers look like in real life! And it all started with a sad-looking little droopy twig.

That's one of the really cool things about perennials. They can fill a number of roles in the garden. You can get them in a variety of shapes, forms, and colors – whether they're chunky or elegant, variegated or colorful leaves, sprawling stems or upright, billowing and carefree or architecturally perfect. Perennials grow in all kinds of conditions, whether it's shade, desert, heat, or cold, and build the background of beautiful borders. Perennials can provide four-season beauty, and they grow stronger by the season. Perennials promise all these things – and they deliver.

At the end of the spring season, when things were slowing down, I was hanging around the garden center one day with my boss and co-worker, just talking. I said, "You know what? I think I'm going to go back to school. And this time, I'm going to major in horticulture. You guys want to come with me?"

"Sure!" they said.

We ended up commuting to school together and took horticulture classes together, and I finally graduated four years later, or close enough. (I minored in writing, naturally.) So, again, perennials turned out to be very helpful. I did my senior thesis on English gardens and totally snowed my Senior Studies professor. He was an Ag man who didn't know much about gardening, so I got an A.

Shortly thereafter, I got a job as city horticulturist. I had a million gardens to plant in the spring. I planted annuals everywhere, but boy, that repetitive motion really hurt my hands and wrists. I used a trowel. Then I tried using bulb planters, which were not effective in the clayey soils in city gardens. Finally I used a little child's shovel to dig a series of holes, then dropped the annuals in and covered them up, in order to save my hands and wrists from all that digging. But this was a lot of labor in spring, and I was always so far behind on all the tasks that needed tending to.

So that fall, I bought a bunch of cheap perennials (everything goes on sale in the fall), wrote down the colors and blooming times for them so I could sort out what would look best where, and then I put them in various gardens to fill out the borders. A one-time planting saved a lot of time and trouble in the spring. Once the perennials filled out and started doing their thing, I didn't have to plant so many annuals, which eased my workload. Now I could do all the other things that needed done, which I couldn't do before because I had been planting annuals.

Oh, and I was a one-woman crew for the whole city. I was assigned inmate labor, but I couldn't send them off by themselves to work on other gardens – too bad. Or I'd get somebody doing community service, which was more of a babysitting job – decidedly unhelpful! At least in the summer I had a very helpful seasonal worker, and how I wish I could have had her working with me in early spring and early fall. But you can't have everything, I suppose.

I had perennials going in everywhere, even in the rose garden, for extra color and to give me an easier time in general. The nice thing was, in fall I could divide the perennials, then plant them out and have many more perennials. I could gather the seeds in October and November, when I was cleaning up the gardens, and plant them in the greenhouse to spread around the parks next spring. Your taxpayer dollars at work.

Anyway, this is why I am such a big fan of perennials. In recent years, roses have pretty much eclipsed perennials for me, These days, I'm starting to come back around to perennials again. They're easy to take care of, they offer a multitude of forms and shapes and sizes and colors and blooming times, and once they're in the ground, they're pretty good about growing for a long time. They got me into my major in college (finally), they saved me a lot of time as a horticulturist, and they look good. All in all, a very, very helpful kind of plant to have.

This book will show you around this fascinating world of perennials. I'll show you how to figure out what you need in your garden by looking at what your garden has to offer your plants in terms of site, the amount of sunlight and rain it gets, and ways to improve the soil for best results. I'll talk about garden design (because with perennials, you work with not only color, but coordinating bloom times for all-season color), how to care for your perennials, how to keep them looking good through the year, and ways to troubleshoot your garden problems, whether it's insect pests, diseases, animals, or weeds.

Welcome aboard!

Hey, if you have any ideas for future books, or see something I've missed in this book that you'd like to see covered, drop me a line at rosefiend@gmail.com and I'll get right on it. Also, if you want to subscribe to my newsletter, go to my website and sign up at melindacordell.com. Then you'll always know when my next book will be coming out. You can also help me choose upcoming topics, book covers, and I'll give you free chapters, book samples, and gardening tips. Enjoy!

Me about age 5 with a trowel and cosmos.

ABOUT THE AUTHOR

Melinda R. Cordell worked in most all aspects of horticulture – in garden centers, in wholesale greenhouses, as a landscape designer, and finally as city horticulturist, where she took care of who-knows-how-many-gardens around the city as well as the Krug Park rose garden and the 300 roses there. She fought the rose rosette virus, which killed off over 50 roses during her very first year, and planted both old and new varieties, using mostly organic methods. She lives in northwest Missouri with her husband and kids, the best little family that ever walked the earth, as well as two hens and a couple roses and a lot of weeds. She hates weeding so much. You can't even imagine. She also wrote *Courageous Women of the Civil War: Soldiers, Spies, Medics, and More; Angel in the Whirlwind; Those Black Wings, Butterfly Chaos,* and *Don't Throw In the Trowel: Vegetable Gardening Month by Month.*

If you like this book, please leave a review on my Amazon or Goodreads page. Reviews help me get more readers. Be sure to recommend my books to any of your gardener friends (and even your gardener enemies).

Thank you so much for reading.

Made in the USA
Columbia, SC
24 November 2020

25395735R00083